The Palgrave Lacan Series

Series Editors
Calum Neill
Edinburgh Napier University,
Edinburgh, UK

Derek Hook
Duquesne University
Pittsburgh, USA

Jacques Lacan is one of the most important and influential thinkers of the 20th century. The reach of this influence continues to grow as we settle into the 21st century, the resonance of Lacan's thought arguably only beginning now to be properly felt, both in terms of its application to clinical matters and in its application to a range of human activities and interests. The Palgrave Lacan Series is a book series for the best new writing in the Lacanian field, giving voice to the leading writers of a new generation of Lacanian thought. The series will comprise original monographs and thematic, multi-authored collections. The books in the series will explore aspects of Lacan's theory from new perspectives and with original insights. There will be books focused on particular areas of or issues in clinical work. There will be books focused on applying Lacanian theory to areas and issues beyond the clinic, to matters of society, politics, the arts and culture. Each book, whatever its particular concern, will work to expand our understanding of Lacan's theory and its value in the 21st century.

Bruce Fink

Lacan on Desire

Reading Seminar VI

palgrave
macmillan

Bruce Fink
McKees Rocks, PA, USA

ISSN 2946-4196 ISSN 2946-420X (electronic)
The Palgrave Lacan Series
ISBN 978-3-031-76385-4 ISBN 978-3-031-76386-1 (eBook)
https://doi.org/10.1007/978-3-031-76386-1

This Palgrave Macmillan imprint is published by the registered company Springer Nature Switzerland AG.
The registered company address is: Gewerbestrasse 11, 6330 Cham, Switzerland

If disposing of this product, please recycle the paper.

To Héloïse, as always

Bibliographical Note

All works are referred to here with the standard format of the author's last name, year of publication, and page number. Exceptions have been made, however, for (1) the *Standard Edition of the Complete Psychological Works of Sigmund Freud*, vols. I–XXIV (London: Hogarth Press, 1953–1974), referenced here simply by volume and page number (e.g., SE XIII, p. 23); and for (2) *The Seminar of Jacques Lacan*, not all volumes of which are available yet in either French or English. When available in print, they are referenced by Seminar (abbreviated S) and page number (e.g., S11, p. 23); when unpublished, they are referenced by Seminar and date of class (e.g., S13, class given on November 11, 1965). I do not always adopt the translations given in the current English editions. A further exception has been made for (3) Lacan's *Écrits*, which is cited repeatedly; the page numbers given here refer to *Écrits: The First Complete Edition in English* (New York & London: W. W. Norton & Co., 2006). Full references are given directly in the Translator's Notes to Seminar VI included in the Appendix, since they are designed to be read alongside the Seminar.

In referring to Shakespeare's *Hamlet*, I include the standard Act, Scene, and Line numbers in parentheses (e.g., V, ii, 12).

A bibliography of Lacan's Seminars cited here and a full reference section are found at the end of the volume.

Preface

What all of the subjects who contact us have in common is that they distrust their desire.
—Lacan (S6, p. 447)

Why devote a whole year's course on psychoanalysis to desire? Is it one of the fundamental concepts of psychoanalysis? The term is rarely found in English translations of Freud's work, although it is obviously related to Freud's term *Wunsch*, which is usually translated into English as "wish" and into French as *voeu*. *Voeu* is a rather weak term, and indeed a bit pious, used as it is in religious contexts to mean vow, promise, or pledge. (The verb that corresponds to *voeu*, *vouloir*, is not especially weak, but its other noun form is *volonté*, "will," which tends to lead off in another, often philosophical, direction.) Another possible translation of *Wunsch* into French would be *souhait*, again a fairly tame term often used reverentially.

Lacan prefers the French term *désir* because it packs a punch, it being pronounced more emphatically. He goes so far, in "Direction of the Treatment" (*Écrits*, p. 518), as to liken the sound of *Wunsch* in German and of "wish" in English "to the sound of damp firecrackers" that "fizzle out" in a way that "suggests anything but concupiscence." It is hard to imagine talking about a *voeu sexuel* or a *souhait sexuel* in French. Well, it can be imagined, but no one says it! *Désir* is thus the term Lacan generally adopts to translate Freud's *Wunsch*, but this also entails a certain substitution of one signifier for another, the replacement of a Freudian term by a Lacanian one; for Freud had, I believe, other German terms available to him (*Lust*, *Begierde*, etc.), but did not employ them in the contexts in which Lacan employs "desire." (Lacan does much the same thing with Freud's terms *Lust*, "pleasure," and *Befriedigung*, "satisfaction," substituting the stronger French term *jouissance* for them.)

Lacan claims that there is an important difference between Freud's *Wunsch* and his term *désir*: "*Wunsch* is not, in and of itself, *désir*; it is a formulated or articulated desire" (S6, p. 37).[1] So *Wunsch* includes a little more and a little less than *désir*: more articulation and less punch.

Wunsch is arguably a very important concept in Freud's work—emphasized in the contexts of dreams, daydreams, fantasies, and symptom formation, to name just a few—and thus desire (a.k.a. wishing or wanting) would seem to be a major concept in psychoanalysis more generally; yet it was rarely talked about in Lacan's time, analysts focusing instead on fantasy (above all, Melanie Klein's version of fantasy), object relations, and the ego.

Now what does Lacan tell us about desire? He says that "desire presents itself as a torment to man" (S6, p. 359), a claim that could not easily be made using the terms *voeu*, *souhait*, or "wish." Desire as a torment was a common theme in Antiquity, especially among the Stoics, and still is in certain Asian traditions in which desire and striving are viewed as the major sources of human suffering. Lacan even quips at one point that "there is no other discontent in civilization than the discontent of desire" (p. 412). Reason enough to delve into the topic!

By way of a spoiler, or a disclaimer, let me point out that after giving this Seminar for eight months (which for his readers comes after 470 pages), Lacan admits that "it has not been easy to pinpoint the place of desire" (S6, p. 471). In other words, by the end of the Seminar, he does not feel that he has conclusively located desire, whatever that means

---

[1] Cf. Lacan's (2001) comment: "It is significant that in Freud's work desire only goes by the name of *Wunsch*. *Wunsch*, wish, is *souhait*. A *souhait* is always enunciated. Desire is only present beneath [or: behind] demand" ("Il est significatif que dans Freud le désir ne se produise jamais que du nom de *Wunsch*. *Wunsch*, wish, c'est le souhait. Il n'y a de souhait qu'énoncé. Le désir n'est présent que sous la demande"; p. 356).

(perhaps he means on the Graph of Desire, but it seems to be a more general comment in that context). This is undoubtedly true of most of his Seminars: few people come away from reading Seminar IV with the sense that he definitively formulated the structure of phobia in it, that by the end of Seminar VIII he decisively formulated the nature of love and transference, and so on. New formulations regarding each of the topics taken up in the Seminars are found in his later work, adding successive layers to his discussions of them. Definitive statements are endlessly deferred.

I assume throughout that the reader is reading the corresponding sections of Seminar VI alongside my exploration of them here.[2]

McKees Rocks, PA, USA   Bruce Fink

---

[2] This book is based on a seminar that I gave in a number of places: Paris, May 19–20, 2023; Ghent, July 14–15, 2023; Belgrade, May 18–19, 2024; and Auckland, November 30–December 1, 2024. An early version of the first 20 pages here was presented as "Objects Lost and Found" to Lacan Toronto on November 15, 2020, by Zoom. All of the material included here was supposed to have been outlined in Copenhagen in September 2020 and Ghent 2021; both events were canceled owing to border and other complications arising from the so-called pandemic.

Praise for *Lacan on Desire*

"This extraordinary introduction to Lacan's thinking starts with the clarification of 'desire,' but then expands into a comprehensive, clear, and profound review of Lacan's entire body of psychoanalytic theory, including its relationship to psychoanalytic techniques and a very detailed analysis of the Lacanian clinical approach. There is no other text that I know of that approaches the problem of translating Lacan's formulations in such a perfect way, making it available to the psychoanalytically informed reader. It provides new focus and depth to contemporary controversies and conflicts in psychoanalytic thinking and closes a major persisting gap in the interchange of psychoanalytic science and profession."

—Otto Kernberg, *Professor Emeritus, Weill Cornell Medical College, New York*

"In this book, Lacan scholar and psychoanalyst Bruce Fink delves into one of the seminars he translated: *Desire and Its Interpretation*. He does not seek to accurately phrase what Lacan said, but rather explains and contextualizes the key problems Lacan was working on during that era of his teaching. The book not only serves as a guide to reading the seminar; it also provides an outstanding standalone discussion of core questions and concepts in Lacanian psychoanalysis."

—Stijn Vanheule, *Ghent University*, author of *Why Psychosis Is Not So Crazy*

"Why don't we want what we want? In this eloquent guide to one of Lacan's most important and misunderstood concepts, Bruce Fink blends clinical insight and theoretical clarity, shedding light on what animates us, our torment, our passion—desire. Written in accessible prose, this book explores Lacan's seminar on *Desire and Its Interpretation,* making it an indispensable resource. Fink turns desire inside out, showing how Lacan pushes Freud beyond the Oedipal. This compelling book not only serves as a valuable companion to Lacan's seminar but also provides profound clinical insights into the complex nature of desire, thus appealing to students as well as practitioners."

—Patricia Gherovici, psychoanalyst and author
of *Transgender Psychoanalysis*

Contents

List of Figures

Part I

Theoretical Backdrop

1

What Is Desire?

We will begin our theoretical discussion of desire with the basics. Lacan states right at the outset that desire is "riveted to a certain linguistic function—that is, to a certain relationship between the subject and the signifying system" (S6, p. 5). In other words, what he refers to as desire is not what we find in the animal kingdom, even though we loosely say that the cat *wants* to go out or that the dog *wants* its bone. Wanting in the animal kingdom is not the same as wanting in the human realm. Human wants are colored, structured, and indeed skewed (i.e., distorted) by language. (Here we might say that Lacan is incorporating the "articulated" nature of Freud's *Wunsch* into his term *désir*.)

We are, of course, animals in some sense, and we have needs just like they do. What distinguishes us from most other animals is the fact that we are born into a world in which virtually everyone around us speaks and expects us to learn to speak. We have certain obvious needs which they are able to attend to and satisfy more or less effectively, but in the course of time we experience discomforts—we may be too hot or too cold, thirsty, hungry, wet, in pain, anxious, or simply lonely—that they cannot divine, and they encourage or even oblige us to put our needs and discomforts into words.

© The Author(s), under exclusive license to Springer Nature Switzerland AG 2025
B. Fink, *Lacan on Desire*, The Palgrave Lacan Series,
https://doi.org/10.1007/978-3-031-76386-1_1

Language Radically Transforms Our Needs

> Need is caught up, modified, and identified in demand.
> —Lacan, S6, p. 196

This, according to Lacan, leads to a radical transformation of our needs. And this happens for several different reasons.

1. <u>Alienation</u>

First of all, the words in which we learn to express our needs are not of our own making. They are not designed to perfectly express what *we* are feeling or experiencing. They are words that have gained currency over the course of centuries, having been forged and modified by generations of speaking beings. What *those* people wanted to express with the words *they* came up with is not necessarily what *we* want to express, and yet they are the only words we have at our disposal. (We can of course utter nonsense sounds, but no one around us will know what we are asking for.) We must, therefore, force our experience into the funnel or straitjacket of the language spoken by those around us—at least if we hope to receive anything from them. (But even when we do, they often misinterpret us! More on that later.) Lacan often refers here to "the defiles of the signifier"—that is, its narrow straights or passageways.

We know that children experience this funneling as an onerous and sometimes odious task, not simply because pronunciation recognizable to others is often quite difficult for children to achieve—their parents being the only ones who can understand them for quite some time. We know they experience it as an onerous and sometimes odious task because some children *refuse* to funnel their experience into language, having apparently given up all hope of receiving anything worthwhile from those around them. Sometimes they go on strike, in a sense, refusing to speak until or unless they are treated differently by their primary caretakers.[1]

---

[1] Certain caretakers propose one specific object after another to a child, for example a toy, a pacifier, a cookie, and the child simply cries, not knowing how to ask for something else: presence, holding, stroking, etc.

Leaving such children aside (they are known in psychoanalysis as autists),[2] we can say that for most children, expressing their needs in words requires effort and leads to what Lacan refers to as "alienation." He calls it "alienation" because some portion of children's experience is inevitably lost in translation, is inescapably lost because the words their parents make available do not completely fit their experience. Some part of their experience, some aspect of their need, is overlooked or stripped away when put into words familiar to those around them. Some portion of their experience can thus be said to become alienated from them, taken from them by the very process of putting it into words.[3]

This may seem to be a highly abstract notion, so consider our experience learning to express ourselves in a foreign tongue, a language we learn, not as infants, but later in life. Most of us, in learning a second or third language (or, for some, a fourth or fifth language!) grapple, at least at the outset, with the fact that the adjectives and expressions available to us in the new language do not seem to cover the exact same ground as what we wish to convey. Naturally, what we wish to convey seems far easier to express in our mother tongue than in this new language, and our sense of alienation in a new language strikes us especially in the realms of love, hate, and humor.

We feel especially inept and alienated when we attempt to express in the new tongue how we feel to someone with whom we have fallen in love, unable to effectively curse out those who treat us abominably, and especially inept and alienated when we try to joke around or be witty. We feel that our verbal communications of love keep missing the mark, that our expressions of hatred don't hit home, and that our jokes—when we are able to make any at all—seem funny only to ourselves.[4]

Our feeling of alienation in learning to speak a new language is perhaps not so different from the infant's feeling of alienation in learning to speak a first language.[5]

---

[2] See Jean-Claude Maleval (2021), and my forthcoming work commenting on it.

[3] The words we learn to use also sometimes say *more* than we intended to express, not just less.

[4] Imagine trying to say in another tongue something like, "That's when the shit hit the fan!" for example.

[5] The analogy is imperfect, for it assumes that experience precedes language, and this is not at all clear. Having funneled our experience into a mother tongue, the latter then impacts what we come to want to express in the new language.

2. The Addressee

> The nature of demand is to be linguistic, to be articulated.
> —Lacan, S14, p. 415

The first reason why expressing our needs in words leads to a radical transformation of our needs is that the words and expressions we learn to articulate don't exactly fit our experience. The second reason has to do with the addressee—in other words, the person to whom we express our needs.

Lacan introduces a technical term for a need that a child expresses in words: he calls it *une demande*. In English, we would usually translate that as a "request," "demand" being an especially strong request in English, but translators have generally taken the path of least resistance by employing "demand" (I'll use both in what follows). *A demand is thus a need that a child verbally expresses to someone*, someone he or she hopes can satisfy it. *A demand is a need addressed to someone else.*

Now, insofar as I am unable to convey a part of my experience, some facet of my need, in the words I am obliged to use, my addressee can never completely satisfy me. He can satisfy my demand, he can try to give me what I have managed to explicitly ask for, but there will always be a remainder: the part I have *not* managed to put into words. He can, for example, give me a cookie when I say "cookie," but he almost certainly will not give me the exact one I had my eye on or feed it to me in exactly the way I want him to. As Lacan puts it, "There is something displaced in demand, which renders the object demanded incapable of [or: unsuitable for] satisfying desire" (S14, p. 416).

For I want the biggest cookie on the plate, or the one with the most chocolate chips in it. Moreover, I want it fed to me exactly the way my mother fed it to me the day before, with a warm smile and a caress, and since I cannot exactly describe her smile and caress, I am unlikely to receive them from someone else along with the cookie. Even my mother might not feed it to me today the way she fed it to me yesterday, and that might ruin everything. I might end up refusing the cookie and crying my eyes out, and she will have no idea why.

Even when my language skills become more developed, I may still be unable to explain exactly how I want it given to me. "A picture is worth a thousand words," as they say, and even a great poet cannot unambiguously express a facial expression or a caress. Even if I could draw a picture of how I wanted someone to look while feeding me the cookie, everyone sees different things in pictures—just listen some time to people interpreting facial expressions they see in photographs,[6] and in artworks like the *Mona Lisa*! My caregiver would probably interpret my picture differently than I did and put on a face that differs significantly from the one I requested. *Something will always be wanting (or lacking) in the way in which my request is granted. It will never be exactly right.*

According to Lacan, *it is that very leftover*—the very thing that is not expressed in my request and structurally cannot be expressed in my request—*that constitutes desire.* It is the remainder of my experience of need that fails to be fully expressed in words and that persists after my demand is formulated, and even after I have been given what I expressly asked for.

The example I often use is that of a birthday present. Let us imagine that your partner asks you what you'd like for your birthday and you request the latest model iPhone. Your birthday arrives and your partner gives you such an iPhone, but she failed to include all the features you wanted and which you were sure she would have anticipated. Moreover, she got you a white version of the phone whereas you wanted black, and she put it in a plain cardboard box instead of presenting it in pretty wrapping paper with a bow on it. To top it all off, she simply left it near the coffee maker the morning of your birthday, or banged it down on the breakfast table in front of you saying, "Well, here's what you wanted," with no affection in her look or tone of voice.

This example might be used to highlight Lacan's claim that every request is a request for love, every demand is a demand for love. The idea here is that everything we ask for, insofar as we ask for it from another person, involves a relationship with that person, the presence of that person, and what we want and don't want from that person. We are, in that

---

[6] Donna Williams provides quite astonishing interpretations of pictures of herself as a child in her book *Nobody Nowhere* (London: Corgi, 1993), between pages 78 and 79.

sense, always asking for more than meets the eye, or rather more than meets the ear. In many cases, we are even willing to set the need aside altogether if we get the presence and love that we are seeking—for example, I can do without the cookie if I receive the love I am longing for. I can't, naturally, do without food forever, but I can be satisfied without receiving the cookie, and certainly without receiving it this very minute. And I can obviously live without the latest model iPhone, especially if my partner says she really can't afford it right now but puts a lot of thought into an all-day outing for us, inexpensive as it may be.

My partner here succeeds in setting aside what I explicitly requested and focusing instead on what I failed to convey in my request—something latent, something unexpressed and perhaps for me inexpressible. Unable to grant my demand, she nevertheless *reads my desire* and attempts to fulfill it. I might even come away after my birthday thinking she knows me better than I know myself, she knows what I want better than I myself do.

As Lacan puts it, behind every demand we make, there is the Other as presence and absence, as "a subject who provides the gift of love. What he gives is beyond anything he can give. What he gives, he gives by his presence and by his presence alone" (S6, pp. 112–3).

Let us note that young animals, too, address their needs to their parents, but they do not do so in words. Thus they, too, make demands, but they are not articulated demands. Nature has presumably provided young animals with enough range of vocal, visual, and/or tactile expression to convey their basic needs to their caretakers. And when they cannot convey some aspect of their experience—as, for example, if they are suffering from some kind of invisible injury or illness—the fact remains that their parents can do little or nothing for them anyway. The only thing their addressees can do with regard to the experiences they cannot convey is be present, remain with them. And sometimes they do not even do that, sensing perhaps that the youngster is ill and might make those around it ill as well.

We might hypothesize that young animals' needs are quite straightforward, and that their parents are able to completely satisfy the demands they make with their cries and behavior. Even if this is not absolutely true in all cases, we can see that the situation is quite different from very early on in the human world.

Owing to language, children's needs become contaminated, in a sense, by something extraneous. When a young animal is hungry, cries for food, and is presented with food, it eats. To the best of my knowledge, a young foal that has to prod, coax, and cajole its mother into letting it suckle does not feel the experience has been ruined by the effort and refuse to suck and go off to sulk for hours. When a young human being is hungry, cries, and is presented with food, sometimes it does not eat—sometimes it refuses nourishment and broods and mopes instead. Why? Because when we make requests or demands, we are always asking for more than meets the ear, more than what we say. We only accept the food if it is presented in a certain way, just the way we like it, or patiently and with a smile. If a bottle is simply shoved into our mouths, we may push it away even though our stomachs are growling. We may go on a hunger strike and refuse all nourishment until such time as our parents' attitude toward us softens or changes in some other way. (Or we may eat or drink in secret, not wanting to give them the satisfaction of feeling they've done something for us.)

Here we can see that we always want something *more* from the person to whom we address our demands than what is included in biological need alone. We always want something connected to our relationship with the addressee.[7] One facet of this is that we want the addressee to anticipate our wishes so that we don't even have to ask, don't have to make explicit everything we want and how we want it. We want the addressee to read our desire.

As addressees ourselves, we always have a choice when we care for a child or a partner: we can hear every request or demand they make as the straightforward expression of a need—"I need this very specific thing right now"—or we can hear their requests as expressing something more between the lines, as it were. If we repeatedly respond to a child's cry or even words requesting food with food and food alone, we end up conveying that we have no interest in reading its desire, or hearing something

---

[7] This was true of rhesus monkeys, too, that—in Harry Frederick Harlow's experiment—clung to the furry mother even if she provided no food, instead of the cold wire one that did provide food.

that goes beyond caloric nourishment to some other form of nourishment—emotional nourishment!

There are parents who are, owing to their own personalities and childhood experiences, extremely cold to their children, almost never pick them up or hold them, and who attend to their basic physical needs and little else. They are the kinds of parents whose children are most likely to go on a hunger strike; and if not on a hunger strike, to refuse to ever spontaneously or voluntarily empty their bowels, requiring their parents to administer suppositories in the best of cases, and requiring their parents to hospitalize them in the most extreme cases.

3. The Slippery Nature of Language

> Desire can be satisfied with no object, even if there are objects that are causes of desire.
> —Lacan (S14, p. 413)

The third reason why expressing our needs in words leads to a radical transformation of our needs has to do with *the slippery nature of language itself.*

Language by its very nature has a difficult time capturing or truly depicting the objects of need and desire. Lacan refers in *Écrits* to "desire's incompatibility with speech" (p. 641). You are all aware, no doubt, how slippery speech can be.

Let's say that you want to prepare a specific recipe requiring parsley and you ask your partner to pick up some on the way home from work. What does he do? He brings you dried parsley instead of fresh parsley. You were sure he knew you always cook with fresh herbs, not dried ones, so it never even occurred to you to add the word fresh to your request. The next time you ask him for parsley, you remember to say "fresh parsley," and he comes home with one strand of parsley, whereas you expected a large bunch. You assumed he realized that you use a serious quantity of herbs in the dishes you make. The time after that, you tell him to purchase 200 grams of fresh parsley, and he brings home a large bunch of fresh coriander, which looks similar to parsley and which someone had mistakenly placed in the same bin as the parsley. No matter how specific you make your request, something almost inevitably goes wrong!

Smart phones have made some of these misunderstandings less frequent, for husbands often place a video call to their wives while standing in front of the vegetable counter, and show them exactly what is available for purchase on the shelf, but misunderstandings continue to abound in almost every area, especially human relations.[8]

You might think that the more specific you get, the less room there is for misunderstanding, but anyone who has tried to write out foolproof directions to their house or foolproof directions for assembling a piece of furniture knows that they can be misinterpreted at virtually any point. In Paris, Colette Soler once dared the students in her class to come up with a statement that could not possibly be interpreted in more than one way—it was a funny experiment which led to a lot of laughter but no unequivocal statements! Lacan himself once said, "it is impossible to unequivocally pin down any signification whatsoever" (S14, p. 419).[9]

Real human languages, unlike artificial languages, are extremely sloppy, in a sense, being unable to designate something unambiguously, indeed anything unambiguously. There is virtually always room for slippage between what I intend to convey and what my interlocutor hears.

First of all, and as you are all aware, certain spoken sounds can be spelled in more than one way, and my interlocutor may think I said HERE instead of HEAR, and THERE instead of THEIR. This is the problem posed by *homonyms*.

Secondly, between the fact that my pronunciation may not at times be perfect or easy to hear over other ambient noises, and the fact that my interlocutor's hearing may not be all that acute, he may conclude that I said PARTLY instead of PARSLEY, LATELY instead of LASTLY, etc.

Thirdly, *we often hear what we want to hear or are expecting to hear*, and we thus project onto what people say what we are expecting them to say, thereby mishearing them, just like we misread certain signs and written texts. Someone who has never heard of parsley may hear something

---

[8] And smartphones lead to numerous misunderstandings of their own: placing accidental "pocket calls" and encouraging telegraphic-like communications open to myriad interpretations.

[9] *Votre discours en dit toujours plus que ce que vous n'en dites*: "your speech always says more than what you say about it" (S5, p. 12).

completely different in my request for parsley: a request for parsnips, Farsi, or any number of other things, depending on the vocabulary that is familiar to him. Such misunderstandings are especially common when we don't know a language terribly well—we at times substitute words or expressions we do know for those that we don't know, and try to make sense of what people are saying to us on the basis of faulty interpretations of their speech.[10]

Fourthly, the way I express myself is virtually always inherently equivocal, it being almost impossible to say something that cannot be interpreted differently than the way I intended it. Homonyms are one obvious problem, but most human grammars, too, are slippery and equivocal. For example, if I say that "the bomb was to go off two minutes later," you cannot know whether I mean that the bomb was set to explode two minutes later, but didn't go off because it was disarmed, or whether I mean the bomb exploded two minutes later. Lacan discusses this example (from Raymond Queneau) on several occasions. Many facets of grammar, whether in English, French, or virtually any other tongue as well, are potentially ambiguous. A patient of mine once said, "There's no one to help." Did he mean that there was no one to help him or that there was no one for him to help? Totally unclear![11]

Context changes meanings too. "Let him have it" can mean "give some specific object to him" or "hit him with everything you've got." And, of course, almost anything may be meant seriously or ironically (or sarcastically). Consider, for example, lines like "That was the best meal I ever had!" or "That was my finest hour!"

4. Meaning Is Determined by the Other

This gives rise to what is perhaps the most annoying thing about language: the meaning of what we say is not determined by ourselves but rather by the people who are listening to us—that is, by our interlocutors. We intend to say one thing, and our interlocutors hear something

---

[10] Not knowing the French term *décupler* (to increase or multiply), I once thought my interlocutor was saying *découpler* (detach or decouple) and foolishly made a big deal of it.

[11] Other examples include "put him out," which can mean put him outside or inconvenience him, and "get him off," which can mean satisfy him sexually or get him off of you.

else. Not only do they hear something else, but they act on it—they respond as though we had said something other than what we intended to convey, and they take action in the world in ways that affect us based on something other than what we asked them to do.

This bothers most of us our whole lives long! Why can't other people simply understand what I am saying instead of always getting it backwards or hearing something completely extraneous in what I've said? If I tell a classroom full of students that the Renaissance did not begin in the 16th-century but rather in the 15th-century, they will almost certainly overlook the word "not" and believe that it began in the 16th century. When I invite people in France to come to dinner at my house at 7 p.m., they often show up at 8 p.m. And they sometimes even assure me that I said eight. I know perfectly well that I didn't say eight, but that's what they "heard" or at least wanted to hear, perhaps because they were busy until 7:30, or because that's the more usual dinner time.

This dismays most of us, for it implies that our thoughts, feelings, wishes, and intentions are being misunderstood all the time. It implies, moreover, that other people disappoint us all the time, failing to correctly interpret even our most explicit requests. Hence we are disappointed not simply by those who couldn't care less about our requests but even by those who are willing to try to meet our explicit requests.

How, then, can we possibly expect them to correctly interpret *what we can never make explicit*: our desire? It seems almost hopeless that our desires could ever be satisfied by other people. *People misunderstand our plainly stated demands, so how could they possibly grasp our desires that we can only ever convey between the lines?*

Most of us keep hoping nevertheless. But, owing to the school of hard knocks, owing to repeatedly disappointing experience, we eventually accept that the meaning of what we say is beyond our control, that as Lacan puts it, meaning is determined by the Other with a capital *O*: meaning is determined in the place of the Other, in the Other's locus.

Our desire, no matter how hard we try to convey it, seems to remain incommunicable to other people. Although it sometimes does not seem ineffable to us, almost no one else seems to grasp it, no matter how hard we try to explain it. Worse still, we would vastly prefer it if people would decipher our desire without us having to make the effort to explain it in four-part harmony, in every detail. But few are those who are willing to try, and fewer still are those who succeed in doing so.

Lacan goes so far as to say that desire is structurally unsatisfiable, that by its very nature it is incompatible with satisfaction. "Demand alone can be satisfied. Desire has no chance of being satisfied" (S14, p. 416). This predicament leaves most of us at least partly frustrated much of the time.

None of This Applies to Psychosis

This is not true, however, for the portion of the population that does not accept the notion that meaning is determined in the place of the Other. When you work with psychotic patients, you may well be struck by the fact they never seem to see anything ambiguous in what they say and almost never in what you say. As a clinician, you may be very unsure as to what they mean when they speak, but to them the meaning is crystal-clear and they cannot understand how you could possibly misunderstand them. Even though they use idiomatic expressions that can be under-stood in a number of different ways, it seems to them that there is no room for misconstrual. They believe that *they* are the masters of meaning, not you. *They* determine the meaning of what they say, not you or anyone else. They have never granted the power to determine the meaning of their speech to anyone else.

Not even to the unconscious! When neurotics make slips of the tongue, they may blithely gloss over them, but they are often at least slightly dis-turbed by them, wondering why something unintended slipped out just then. On the other hand, when psychotics make slips of the tongue, which is usually quite rare, they grant them no meaning whatsoever. To them, a mistake is just a mistake. No other voice intervened, nothing within themselves spoke, interrupting what they consciously meant to say, and hence there is no meaning that can be attributed to their occa-sional bungled actions.

This implies that they perceive no slippage between what they say and what they mean. Neurotics lament the fact that they often feel unable to convey exactly what they mean, that they can't find the exact words with which to express what they feel, what they are experiencing, and what they think. They may feel that it is clear in their own minds but that they can't find the exact words with which to say it, or they realize that what comes out of their mouths is far more ambiguous than what they thought they were thinking—there having been interference in their speech from some other train of thought, from thinking that is going on at another level, on another stage or scene (Freud's *anderer Schauplatz*; see SE IV, p. 48, and SE V, p. 536), in the unconscious.

At other times, neurotics may find that even in their own minds it is not at all clear what they think and feel. Indeed, many people come to analysis highly confused and conflicted about what they want. They may state right at the outset that they know perfectly well what their parents want from them, what their spouses want from them, and even what their children want from them. But they profess not to know what *they* want, what they themselves desire. They think they want X, but they also don't want X, preferring Y. But Y, too, has certain disadvantages. Then again, there is Z. They can't decide, they go back and forth, endlessly mull over the advantages and disadvantages of each course of action, think certain of their options are less moral than others, will win them less praise than others, and so on.

In the course of analysis, they usually come to realize that they have multiple conflicting motives that make it hard for them to know what they want—at the very least they realize they have unconscious motives that conflict with their conscious motives, preventing them from pursuing what they consciously believe they want. They also come to realize that their actions, inactions, and what comes out of their mouths are often ambiguous, being compromise formations between conscious and unconscious motives.

No such realization is forthcoming with psychotics. What they say is what they mean, period, the end. You can search for recognition on their part of ambiguity in what they say until the cows come home, and all you will manage to do is confuse them as to what you are getting at. The more you fish for the slightest flicker of recognition of ambiguity, the more annoyed they may become at you, or think you are playing some kind of game with them.

To their way of thinking there is no slippage between what they say and what they want, and thus there is no hidden desire lurking in or

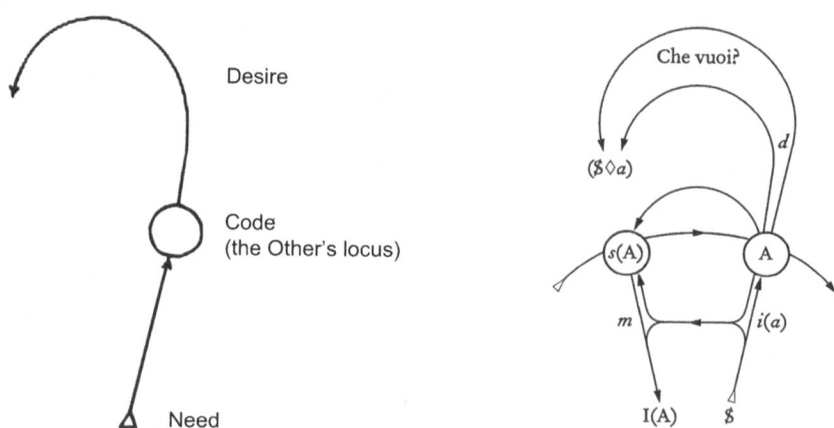

Fig. 1.1 Need, code, desire

behind the requests they make. When neurotics ask to reduce to three sessions a week from four, they are often secretly hoping we will protest and express our desire for them to continue having four sessions a week. Neurotics hope we will see something *beyond the request* in what they say; they hope for an expression of desire from us that the analysis continue at the same intensity, for they can read that as a sign of love, favor, or interest. But when psychotics ask to reduce to three sessions a week from four, they are not secretly hoping we will protest and give a sign of love. There is no slippage, no gap or secret wish lurking between their request and what they actually want.[12]

Desire, as I said earlier, is integrally related to this slippage. When there is no such slippage, there is no place for desire, strictly speaking. Psychotics (and ordinary psychotics too) feel that the words they employ do justice to their experience, that they are able to say exactly what they want, and hence there is nothing left over (see Fig. 1.1), no remainder, that might appear beyond the code, in the form of something left to be desired. (In the Graph of Desire, need encounters the code found in the Other's locus, and desire appears in the upper part of the Graph as what is left

---

[12] Psychotics, too, may want a special sign of our love, but this is not how they will go about seeking it.

over, what is not heard or responded to by the Other. I will comment on the Graph at some length in Chap. 4).

When psychotics are hungry and request to be fed, the food given to them satisfies them. It is not the case with them that there is always something inadequate about what they are given, there is not something that is always a bit off, a bit wrong, a bit out of joint (not at that level, at least).[13]

---

[13] On the rare occasions on which they feel that the words in their mother tongue do not do justice to their experience, they invent words without realizing they have done so. We call these "neologisms," and they appear in certain psychotics' speech without them being aware that other people do not understand them. When we ask them what they mean, they tend to look at us confusedly, being sure we must know. They may then wonder why we are asking. Do we not believe them? Are we accusing them of not speaking in good faith? If we ask too many questions about the meaning of such terms, we may elicit paranoid reactions in them.

We generally have to content ourselves with realizing that the experiences designated by these neologisms are incredibly *meaningful to them*. Psychotics are not often, however, obsessed with trying to communicate them to others, as neurotics usually are, and it generally does not bother psychotics that no one knows what they are talking about, something neurotics usually cannot abide.

2

Fantasy and the Object, or How to Prop up One's Desire

The subject is not where he desires, but … is somewhere in fantasy.
—*Lacan (S6, p. 414)*
Desire is always desire for something else.
—*Lacan (S5, p. 7)*

Since desire is, as we have seen, a remainder or leftover, it can hardly be considered substantial or solid. Virtually no one around us recognizes our desire for what it is, paying heed only to our obvious needs or explicit requests (if those!), finding our hidden or subtler wishes too difficult or annoying to deal with. And we ourselves are often unaware of what we really want. When we perchance have an inkling of what it is, we may well disapprove of it and try not to think about it. As I mentioned earlier, many people seem quite clueless about what they want when they first enter analysis, and it is only thanks to the analyst's questioning and repeating things they say back to them that they begin to listen to themselves and try to decipher what their speech suggests they in fact want. In other words, the desire that inhabits them is often so well hidden from

© The Author(s), under exclusive license to Springer Nature Switzerland AG 2025
B. Fink, *Lacan on Desire*, The Palgrave Lacan Series,
https://doi.org/10.1007/978-3-031-76386-1_2

themselves that they have to listen to themselves speak for a very long time before they can have a sense of what they themselves really want.

The result is that, as human beings, our desire is generally quite fragile and precarious. Yet it is incredibly precious to us—indeed, perhaps, more precious than anything else. Why? Because it goes to the very heart of our subjectivity. That tiny little remainder or leftover is what makes all the difference—it is what distinguishes us from everyone else, and indeed it is what distinguishes us from a machine or a simple extension of our parents.

Lacan, in his usual cryptic way, says some rather mysterious things about desire, one of which is that "desire is the metonymy of being in the subject," which we can slightly amend as "desire is the metonymy of castrated being in the subject," and we can amend it a bit further as "desire is the metonymy of the subject's castrated being" (S6, p. 23). Desire here corresponds to what has been taken away from us, alienated from us, cut away or castrated from us as we expressed our needs in language comprehensible to others, which then reappears (see Fig. 1.1) in a wispy or ghost-like manner at times (above the code, A). Every reappearance of desire relates to the same old thing that we feel we lost. Lacan refers to it as a *metonymy* in the sense that it presents itself first in one form and then in another, the root of which is nevertheless always the same loss, the same alienation or castration. The part of our being that was alienated or castrated as we came into language seeks forever thereafter to appear, to come into being "on the other side," as it were—that is, in the upper part of the Graph.

Lacan even goes so far as to propose here that a wish in a dream is satisfied by "coming into being" (S6, p. 44), that is, by being represented or staged in a dream. According to him, the showing or presenting or re-presenting of the wish in and of itself brings satisfaction with it. My sense is that this is not exactly what Freud means by wish fulfillment, but Lacan clearly thinks that the dreamer is satisfied by coming into being as a wishing or desiring subject. In other words, we find in the dream a subject[1] who wants something and who is satisfied by the staging or presenting of that wanting. Lacan calls this the "desire for desire," or the desire to desire,

---

[1] Lacan brackets this subject (S6, p. 44), and later calls it the unconscious subject (p. 49).

the desire to have a desire—and certain patients complain at various points in their analysis that their desire seems to have waned, to have virtually disappeared, whereas they were full of desire at some earlier time in their lives.[2]

Freud, for his part, places quite a bit of emphasis on the *accomplishment* or *execution* of the wish in a dream, certain dreams in fact presenting the wish as already having come true, as already having been granted: a certain person we hate is already dead; a certain object of our lust is already in bed with us, and indeed the sexual act may not be presented in the dream, but it is clear that it has occurred;[3] the baby one is carrying has already been delivered, and there is no need to go through the painful process of childbirth; and so on.

These are perhaps not incompatible approaches to the notion of wish fulfillment, but it does seem to me that Lacan emphasizes far more the *depiction* of a wish in a dream, whereas Freud emphasizes the (depiction of the) actual execution or *realization* of the wish; indeed, it is often by what is accomplished by the end of the dream that he deduces what the wish must have been.

Patients often complain that in their dreams they seem to be on the verge of realizing a wish or satisfying a desire, but then something goes awry such that they do not get what they want. Freud would retort, "Perhaps you don't really want what you say you want. Perhaps you take a secret pleasure in being dissatisfied, or you feel that wish was not yours, but someone else's, and thus you ensured that it was thwarted in the dream." We could, perhaps, characterize that as *the depiction of a wish to thwart a wish*. Lacan emphasizes that it is precisely where something goes awry in a dream that desire is at work: "Desire is where things go wrong" (S16, p. 170).

What both Freud and Lacan might agree on is that our desires are often unknown to us and find expression primarily in dreams, daydreams, fantasies, and intrusive thoughts.

---

[2] Cf. Ernest Jones' (1961) discussion of "aphanisis" (p. 440).
[3] Note that dreams rarely, if ever, stage the sexual act itself. "There's no such thing as a sexual act," as Lacan puts it in Seminar XIV.

Note that dreams, daydreams, fantasies, and intrusive thoughts are often quickly forgotten and paid little attention to by most people. Indeed, Lacan comments on "How easily we forget *everything* that has to do with the unconscious" (S6, p. 60). This means that for most people, their desire is rarely at the forefront of their attention and is rarely expressed—appearing only occasionally in certain sudden, unexpected, and at times violent actions. Glimpses of our desire are at best fleeting and often disappear as quickly as they appear (just like what I call "the Lacanian subject").[4]

So how, then, do we prop up our desire, support it, make it more solid? We do so through the object. According to Lacan, it is thanks to the object that we manage to keep our desire alive. And this, he would argue, is true even for those who profess not to be aware of what their desire is.

What object are we talking about? The nature of the object in psychoanalysis has been the subject of numerous debates, and there are many different ways of thinking about the object. One of Freud's earliest ways of talking about the object was as one's mother, one's mother as the source of love and sustenance early in life; at times he more specifically referred to the breast as the infant's primary object; and in his discussions of fetishism, he referred to something far more abstract, something he called the "maternal phallus," something that is obviously imagined, not real, but it is something for which the fetishist's object is a substitute.

The Object Is Based on Loss

Something we might note about virtually all of the things that are referred to as "objects" in psychoanalysis is that they are things we have lost in the course of growing up. Let me give a short list of them:

1. Our primary caretaker—usually our mother—as the source of our first satisfactions in life.

---

[4] Cf. Lacan's comment, "Here the subject is stifled and effaced at the very moment he appears. How can some facet of this subject, who disappears as soon as he emerges—produced by a signifier in order to immediately fade [*s'éteindre*] in another—be . . ." (S16, p. 12).

2. Our mother's breast, as the source of our first oral satisfactions in life (for those who were breastfed).[5]

These two have a long and exalted pedigree in psychoanalysis, going by the name of "the lost object," and in both of these cases we are nostalgic for something we never had in exactly the way we later think we had it. For we—or at least some of us—miss what we thought of as exclusive access to our mothers, or at least exclusive possession of her breast, and yet at the time we had not yet come into being as separate subjects from her that could possess something. (What we see on the top, in Fig. 2.1, is not a case of access or possession; what we see on the bottom is.)

Thus we are actually longing for a time in which there was no clear difference between self and other. We are longing for a kind of fusional state prior to our current state of separateness, prior to the differentiation between self and other. Looking back, we imagine ourselves having exclusive access or exclusive possession of something or someone, and yet we had not yet come into existence as subjects capable of possessing anything whatsoever (more accurately put, it is our mothers who possessed us!). Rather than having lost some specific object, we have lost the non-separation between self and other, something Freud perhaps tried to capture with the term "oceanic feeling" in which one feels oneself to be part

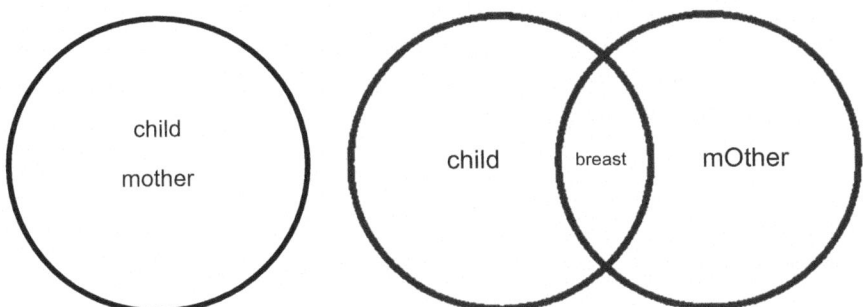

Fig. 2.1 No object versus lost object

---

[5] Lacan says the first object is *not* the breast but the child's thumb (S15, p. 85)!

of a larger whole, an undifferentiated part of the whole universe, or of a specific group of people. Most of us as adults only occasionally feel this under the influence of intense music or psychotropic drugs, if not both at the same time!

In short, the "object" we feel we have lost was not yet an object, as there was not yet any distinction between subject and object. The nostalgia, then, for the lost object is in fact a nostalgia for some "thing" that we in fact never had as a distinct, separate thing.[6]

That said, I will continue to outline what we lose in the course of growing up:

3. Through the process of toilet training we lose the freedom to urinate and defecate anytime, anyplace. After a year or so of life, our bodily functions come increasingly under the scrutiny of parents who regiment our bodies, demanding that we control our bladders and sphincters. What we produce with our bodies is taken away from us, flushed down the toilet, considered by our parents to be noxious waste products. We thus lose an easy, unproblematic, non-neurotic relationship to our urinary and excretory functions and products, and are forced to leave behind the simple pleasure of going whenever we feel the urge.[7]

4. We lose those facets of our experience that we are unable to express in the words available to us in our mother tongue or tongues. As I indicated earlier, Lacan refers to this as our "alienation in language."

5. We lose what we believed to be a privileged position we had with respect to our parents, a position that Freud refers to with some irony as "His Majesty, the baby," but the same goes for baby girls so we could just as well say "Her Majesty, the baby." Therefore, not only do we lose what we considered to be our privileged access to our mothers, but we are forced to reckon with the fact that we are not the be-all and end-all of her existence. She has a life that goes beyond us, she has

---

[6] It is a longing for an object that we in fact never possessed as a fully-fledged object. Lacan even refers to the nostalgia for such an undifferentiated time in psychoanalytic theory as an illusion or mystification (S16, p. 225). See "The Case of the Lost Object" in Fink (2010).

[7] Some, if not all, derive some modicum of jouissance from (with)holding it. Lacan says, at the end of Seminar XIV, that "all that is neurotic essentially takes place in the bathroom" (p. 423); we might add the kitchen or dining room!

interests that do not include us. This realization may be forced upon us by the arrival of a new child in the family, or by our recognition that there is a partner in the picture who takes her attention away from us at certain times—at too many times, we feel. It may also be forced upon us in other ways—by the fact that the mother gives precedence, not to us, but to her work, her friends, her hobbies, her volunteer or charitable activities, or her extended family. In whatever way it is forced upon us, we have to give up our view of ourselves as the most precious object for our mothers, and perhaps for our fathers as well. For we find that our father, too, gives precedence to other children in the family, to his wife, to his work, to his buddies, to his hobbies, to watching sports on television, or even to studying psychoanalysis (it sometimes happens!).

The Phallus

This fifth loss is related to something Freud identified very early on, giving it a rather controversial name, but one which has been taken up by numerous authors. His or her Majesty, the baby, is forced to realize that he or she is *not* the most precious object in the world for the parents, that he or she is not "the phallus."

Freud talked about the child as being in the position of the phallus as part of his theorization that little girls develop penis envy. They notice that their brothers are treated differently from them, better or more indulgently at times, and this is at a time in their development when the only real physiological or anatomical difference they can perceive between boys and girls is that boys have penises. Freud sometimes emphasized the *physical* prominence of the male genitalia, thinking that girls immediately recognized their superiority based on their visual prominence, but one can easily point to the way in which males have historically been privileged in society and in individual families, they being the ones who carry on the family name, and for hundreds of years they being the ones who inherited the lion's share of the family's property and status. In France and other countries as well, no doubt, even when daughters would have been the obvious inheritors of the throne, they were excluded from such positions of power by a specific law referred to as the *Loi salique*. It is easy to understand why a young girl would come to think that the only reason her brother or her male cousin is given more privileges than she is, is that he has a penis and she doesn't. The penis thereby becomes associated with privilege and power.

According to Freud, little *boys* come to feel that their mothers prefer their fathers to them because the fathers have bigger penises—and this may plague them their entire lives, they continuing to feel, even when they are adults, that their penises are too small, that real men have bigger ones (porn videos on the Internet have only made this worse).[8] And, according to Freud, girls come to feel that they have been altogether deprived of something of great importance.

Freud went on to say that a little girl playing with her dolls imagines that they are babies she has gotten from her father, and that they are somehow substitutes for the penis she was deprived of. To Freud's way of thinking, later in life women look forward to having real children of their own, feeling them to be in some sense substitutes for the penises they never had. This is how he explains the incredible importance granted to children, and especially male children, by so many women; they relish the idea of giving birth to boys who will someday carry on the family name and wield power, and whose power they can thus enjoy vicariously. (This is not true of all women, of course, there being some women who are not terribly interested in males, other women not being terribly interested in any of the children they bring into the world….)

For many women, according to Freud, a child—whether male or female—is a kind of phallic object, a kind of penis substitute, and the importance they grant the child is obviously communicated to the child in a variety of different ways. In its first year of life, a child can—without too much self-deception, perhaps—think of itself (to whatever degree it can be said to think) as that which is most precious to its mother. It is only later forced to revise that view and give up the image of itself as her precious little object—especially as she begins to make more and more

---

[8] I believe it was Kurt Vonnegut who wrote a story in which an invading force from another planet put up billboards everywhere on Earth saying that the average adult human penis size was far larger than it actually is; they were able to conquer Earth with no problem!

demands upon the child: weaning, toilet training, language learning, going to school, table manners, and so on. What might first have been experienced as a kind of unconditional love and acceptance turns into highly conditional love and often disapproving attitudes. The child learns that the mother puts other people, social respectability and standing, education, and perhaps numerous other things first, ranking them more important than her child's wishes and comfort. In such cases, the child is forced to give up what it believed to be its privileged position; it is forced to reckon with the fact that it is not the phallus for the mother (and perhaps never actually was).

Freud, of course, realized that a child is not always ousted from that position. Not every mother privileges something more highly than her child. Not every mother gives precedence to someone or something else. Some mothers continue for an extremely long time, if not forever, to have the child sleep in the parental bed, chasing the partner into another bedroom or onto the living room couch. Some mothers continue to make their child number one in their lives, and make endless excuses for their child who repeatedly fails out of different schools and later cannot hold down a job. They always consider it to be a teacher's fault or a boss' fault—somebody else's fault. The child is perfect, and can bear no blame in the mother's eyes for anything that happens.

Freud's case of little Hans presents us with such a situation. Hans' mother prefers to have her little boy in bed with her to having her husband there; she lets Hans do whatever he wants even when his father disapproves; and she seems to make Hans the center of her universe.[9]

Lacan articulates what happens in such cases as follows: the boy gets stuck *being* the phallus and can never effectively leave behind that position. In the best of cases, a boy gives up on being the phallus and is able

---

[9] When, on the other hand, the child has a mother who gives precedence to other things than her child, who, as Lacan puts it, "already has a certain relationship to the phallus" (S6, p. 213), the child can only manage to get himself valued by entering into competition with the phallus, which in most cases means with the father who he believes is the object of the mother's love and attention. The male child rivals with his father for his mother, but he eventually realizes that he cannot win that competition, and will be castrated by the father should he persist. This is what leads him to give up his mother as his primary love object and identify with his father. (He may, however, redirect his love to his father and wish to take his mother's place in his father's bed; he may then fantasize about anal sex.)

to go on to *have* the phallus by identifying with his father as someone who has some modicum of social status and power.

Giving up on *being* the phallus allows the boy to be able to wield the phallus, and one way we see this is in the use he makes of his penis in sexual relations. The penis as a biological organ is obviously not the same thing as the phallus as a symbol or signifier, and Lacan's vocabulary can be confusing, because he often says "phallus" when he obviously means "penis" (note, however, that "phallus" does mean penis in biological and medical contexts, and Lacan employs a good deal of medical terminology). We see in clinical work that a man who is (to a greater or lesser degree) stuck in the position of *being the phallus* for his mother is often unable to *have erections*, or maintain erections with people he sexually desires, whether men or women.[10] Nothing unusual has happened to his penis, physiologically speaking—for example, it works just fine when he masturbates—but its use in sexual relations is stymied, blocked, nil. Such men often express a sense they have that their penises do not belong to them but rather to their mothers. Hence they cannot use them as they see fit, they cannot use them as they might like to, for they do not perform as planned or hoped.

According to Lacan, there is a choice to be made: one can either be the phallus or have the phallus, but not both at the same time:[11]

> Being and having do not arise at the same stage of identification [...]. There is a true dividing line between the two: one cannot both be the phallus and have it. In order for the subject, under certain conditions, to come to have it, he must give up on being it. (S6, p. 213)

If, for whatever set of complex reasons related to relationships with his parents, a boy is able to and prefers to remain in the position of the most precious object for his mother, he will never identify with his father (or

---

[10] He may go soft or ejaculate at the very moment of penetration.

[11] This is not true in the case of perversion (S6, p. 464); the pervert has it in the form of a fetish or an idol, for example, Gide's wife. This is an example of what I call his "both/and logic": he can both be it and have it. On being and having, see "Guiding Remarks for a Convention on Female Sexuality" (*Écrits*, pp. 725–36).

some other father figure) as someone who possesses the phallus, wields the phallus, and is a force to be reckoned with to his wife and children.

Note, nevertheless, that immediately after saying that, Lacan adds:

> The subject both is and is not the phallus. He *is* it, because it is the signifier with which language designates him, and he *is not* it inasmuch as language and the law of language take it away from him. (S6, p. 214)[12]

Hamlet is certainly depicted by Lacan in this Seminar as someone who cannot wield the phallus. He is perhaps at first viewed by Lacan as the phallus for his mother; then Ophelia takes on the role of the phallus, and finally Hamlet can wield it. (We'll see how and when in Chap. 8.)

There are, of course, many fathers who are *incapable* of wielding the phallus, who are quite impotent with their wives and families, and some who even believe that that is the way it should be. Such fathers hardly inspire their sons to give up the position of being the phallus for their mothers, even in cases where their mothers do not overly encourage their sons to remain in that position. But mothers may point the way for sons with such fathers, for even if they do not swoon over their husbands, they may make it clear that they fantasize about other men who embody the phallus for them—whether Clint Eastwood, Robert Redford, Harrison Ford, Tom Cruise, a family relative, or their own father. In other words, such mothers have a relationship to the phallus that goes well beyond their child: they "already have a certain relationship to the phallus" (S6, p. 213).

Being and having are obviously two of the most important auxiliary verbs or helping verbs, at least in French and English, and in the 1950s Lacan attempts to articulate what men and women need to do with respect to the phallus using these two different verbs. (In the 1970s, he articulates things differently, using various forms of negation identified in logic.) He argues here (S6, p. 213) that "being and having do not arise at the same stage of identification" (*being* presumably comes first, at the imaginary stage of identification, *having* coming later when one perceives

---

[12] In Seminar XVIII, Lacan says that both boys and girls "are the phallus for a little while" (S18, p. 25)—that is, early on in life.

that the father in the family possesses and wields symbolic status and power).

Men, Lacan says, need to give up being the phallus in order to have it (men are "not without having it," as he puts it; S6, pp. 214–5).[13] "Insofar as [a man is the phallus], he does not have it ["he has no right to use it" (p. 450)], and insofar as he has it, he is not it" (p. 445). "It is around the subjective assumption that is inflected between being and having... that the reality of castration is played out." In other words, a man must submit to *castration—to the loss of his position as being the phallus for his mother* (whether fantasized or not)—in order to accede to a position in which he can seek and someday have status and power in the world outside the home.

What about women? Since they do not have a penis, and thus cannot wield it as a symbolic object, they are destined to *be* (or at least represent) the phallus to the men around them; they must "*be [it] without having it.*" The female subject, he says, "*is* without having it" (S6, pp. 214–5). However, Lacan suggests that in the unconscious, women

---

[13] If a woman identifies strongly with being the phallus—that is, representing or embodying it as some sort of *ideal image of femininity* as defined in a specific culture—then she will most likely feel blocked from pursuing status in any other way, for example, in the form of knowledge, musical or artistic talent, wittiness, writing ability, etc. These latter pursuits could be understood as quests to acquire the symbolic phallus, to acquire prestige and status in the eyes of the world.

Some seek to acquire such status through a partner or spouse who they believe has something phallic about him (or her); this is their way of attempting to *have* the phallus. Some may also do it through their children, feeling they acquire higher status because of their beautiful and/or successful children.

Having the phallus concerns the symbolic phallus (Φ) and involves putting the symbolic phallus in the place of the imaginary phallus (the imaginary phallus, $-\varphi$, being related to all the losses discussed in Chap. 3).

$$\frac{\Phi}{-\varphi}$$

This is supposed to be the payoff. We sacrifice jouissance ($-\varphi$) in order to acquire something "better," a different kind of jouissance (Φ).

Being the phallus privileges the imaginary over the symbolic. It involves being stuck attempting to present a certain *image* to the world: "when a woman takes herself to be capital Phi ... she is, of course, frigid" (S15, p. 176). For a man, being the phallus for his mother also tends to make him stuck in a position in which it is hard to seek *symbolic* success in the world.

"both are it and have it" (p. 448).[14] Yet he had already said that of both men and women (p. 214), so go figure!

---

[14] As regards the sense that the phallus is a "detachable object" that may be cut off, he discusses the penis and "what corresponds to it in women" in the same breath, as if girls, too, imagine that their main source of jouissance, the clitoris, could be cut off (S6, p. 482). As we know, clitorectomy (also called female circumcision, female genital mutilation, or female genital cutting) is practiced in certain countries, or at least was practiced up until not very long ago. The reader can find Lacan's main discussion of being and having in Seminar VI on pages 214–5.

3

The Phallus as Loss

There is much that could be said about these formulations about being versus having the phallus, but let us focus first on the general theme of loss. "Human beings," Lacan suggests, "cannot help but consider themselves to be … missing something" (S6, p. 218).[1] To be missing what? We have now enumerated quite a few things we feel we are missing, quite a series of losses: mom, breast, urine, feces, experience forced into words, and his/her Majesty the baby. Which we might recast as our primary caretaker, weaning, toilet training, alienation in language, and being the most precious object.[2]

Lacan proposes that all of these losses become associated with each other, and that they are all lumped together, in a sense, becoming identified with the phallus. What is complicated here in Lacan's work is that the phallus takes on at least two different forms. The one we are beginning with here is the phallus as something lost, as what he terms minus phi $(-\varphi)$. It is the phallus insofar as it is associated with the loss of jouissance.

---

[1] This is the epigraph I chose for my recent collection entitled *Miss-ing* (Fink 2024).

[2] Despite such monumental losses, we can perhaps console ourselves with Diogenes Laertius' delightfully silly formulation: "If you have not lost something, you still have it. But you have not lost horns. Therefore you still have them." See Malpass and Marfori (2017), p. 68.

© The Author(s), under exclusive license to Springer Nature Switzerland AG 2025
B. Fink, *Lacan on Desire*, The Palgrave Lacan Series,
https://doi.org/10.1007/978-3-031-76386-1_3

It is thus a negative value, a negative quantity. (The child, male or female, can imagine losing what seems to be quite an important source of pleasure—the penis or clitoris—having already lost a number of other sources of pleasure.)

How do losses become associated with the phallus? One way of thinking about it is via the castration complex in boys. As Freud propounds it, a boy is presented with a choice: he either gives up his mother as his primary object of love and affection, or he will be castrated by his rival, his father. He thus has to make a calculation: which is more important to him, his mother or his penis? (That is, which is more important to him, his childhood masturbation while thinking about his mother or his penis?) This is one way of thinking about how some sort of equivalence between the mother and the penis or, more generally speaking, the object and the phallus becomes established.

As Lacan puts it, "the subject's penis [is] weighed in the balance against the object, and [takes] on a certain function as an equivalent or standard in the relationship with the object.... It is to the degree to which he gives up his relationship to the phallus [i.e., gives up on being the phallus] that the subject can possess the infinity of objects that characterize the human world" (S6, p. 214). "The penis is restored to a man by a certain action that one can almost say deprives him of it" (p. 215). In other words, it is by allowing himself to be deprived of the position of *being* the phallus for his mother that he is able to in some sense *have* the phallus, be able to use his penis in sexual relations with other people.

(This might well remind us of a formulation one finds in the New Testament: "whoever would save his life will lose it, but whoever loses his life for my sake will find it" [Matthew 16:25]).

"The subject cannot situate himself in desire without castrating himself—in other words, without losing what is most essential about his life" (S6, p. 372). He has to give up the relationship with mom which allowed him to see himself as the phallus, and in which she appeared as his main source of jouissance.

Note that the phallus takes on dozens of meanings in Lacan's work (only a few of which I will list here):

- The bar between the signifier and the signified: S/s (S20, p. 39).
- The only *Bedeutung* (signification or signifierness) in all of language (S18, p. 128).
- The Name-of-the-Father (this apparently scandalized certain people; see S18, pp. 25 and 151).
- It is semblance itself (S18, p. 132), which is also equated with S_1 in the master's discourse.
- It is an obstacle to any relationship between man and woman (man and man, woman and woman too; S18, p. 53).
- "The phallus is quite clearly sexual jouissance insofar as it is coordinated with semblance, insofar as it is part and parcel of semblance" (S18, p. 25).

I won't try to make those *later* formulations comprehensible here, focusing instead on how Lacan presents the phallus in Seminar VI.

The Object (Our Partner) Embodies All Losses

What Lacan goes on to propose—and this is just one approximate way of putting it—is that, once we have given up mom, the next person who comes to occupy the position of our object of desire somehow embodies, covers over, and yet represents the whole set of losses I listed above. That person takes the place of the lost jouissance, and we hope to recover the lost jouissance through him or her. This is what leads Lacan to say that the object contains within itself the phallus as lost (see, for example, S6, pp. 213 and 327, where the following "formula" is implicit), which we can write as follows:

$$\frac{a}{-\varphi}$$

This "formula" is implied very directly when Lacan says, "The object ... takes the place ... of what the subject is deprived of symbolically" (S6, p. 312).[3]

The first object that he puts in this position is our little brothers or sisters insofar as they are our rivals—rivals for our mother's attention. Recall Lacan's repeated references to St. Augustine's statement: "I myself have seen and known an infant to be jealous even though it could not [yet] speak. It became pale, and cast bitter looks on its foster-brother."

Lacan comments on it as follows:

> Thus Augustine forever ties the situation of spectacular absorption (the child observed), the emotional reaction (pale), and the reactivation of images of primordial frustration (with an envenomed look)—which are the psychical and somatic coordinates of the earliest aggressiveness—to the infant (preverbal) stage of early childhood. (*Écrits*, p. 93)

In such cases, children feel that it is their siblings who deprive them of their mother and of her breast and other forms of care (S6, p. 219). Indeed, the breast first becomes perceived to be an object of extreme value when it is taken away from the child and given to another child. Moreover, when children look at their rivals, they cannot help but think of the enjoyment they feel they have lost because of them. The little other, which is what Lacan at first calls little object *a*, has what they want, has the enjoyment they feel they are now missing out on. There may appear to be two objects here, the breast and the rival, but *the rival takes on the significance of the breast insofar as it is the rival who now has it*. This little other comes to represent the jouissance I feel I am missing out on: minus phi $(-\varphi)$.

A considerable portion of our libidinal investment in our mothers now becomes bound up with our rival, transferred to our rival. Early on in his work, Lacan even considered this to be one of the possible pathways toward homosexuality, a bitter rivalry with a sibling of the same sex

---

[3] In Seminar XVI, Lacan, using the golden mean for *a*, suggests that all of the subject's losses add up to *a*. Each loss is an even power of *a*. His formula is as follows:

$$a = a^2 + a^4 + a^6 \ldots$$

leading to an intense libidinal love/hate relationship with that same sibling and then later in life with someone like him or her.

One of my patients was about three years old when his younger brother was born, and my patient felt intensely jealous of him and deprived of his mother as soon as the brother arrived on the scene. He had a highly aggressive and hateful relationship with his brother his entire life. Their father died when the two of them were in their forties, and when they were splitting up the belongings he had left to them, my patient deliberately selected things he did not want but that he believed his brother would want, just to annoy his brother. Even in his late forties, he still wanted to deprive his brother, just like he felt he had been deprived of so many things by his brother early in life.

Whenever he thinks of his brother, even now in his 50s, he imagines killing him and resents everything that his brother has, including his relationship with their elderly mother. To him, his brother represents everything he feels he has lost. He imagines that he had it really good up until the time of his brother's birth, and that the whole rest of his life was a disaster. (Ironically enough, his mother said that she decided to have a second child because my patient seemed so lonely and she thought he would be happier if he had a playmate!)

We might refer to this rival as the first form of the partner, as we see him or her later in life. It is not clear whether the subject *consciously* hopes to recover any of that lost jouissance through the partner, through his or her relationship to the partner; yet there is a surreptitious recovery of some of the jouissance via the rivalrous relationship itself. And certainly there is a perception on the subject's part that the partner/rival contains, embodies, or somehow represents the jouissance he feels he has lost.

One of my female analysands has a very similar relationship to her younger brother, born when she was two and a half years old, as the abovementioned male analysand has to his younger sibling. Even now, in middle age, she always feels that he gets much more from the family in every regard than she does—money, attention, and respect—even though she has accomplished a great deal more than he has. Prior to his birth, she was the apple of her parents' eye, but ever since he came on the scene she has felt ousted from that position and holds him personally responsible for that. Even today, she cannot see him or even think of him without resentment. And, not that surprisingly, some of that resentment and rivalry appears in her relationship with her husband as well.

Regarding the matheme −φ, Lacan refers to it as:

> what Freud pinpointed as essential in the mark left on man by his relation to logos—that is, castration, which is, in effect, assumed [*assumée*] here at the imaginary level. This notation will allow us to define desire's object *a* as it appears in our formulation of fantasy [...]
>
> Desire's object *a* is the object that sustains the relationship between the subject and what he is not [...] *insofar as he is not the phallus.*
>
> Object *a* sustains the subject in the privileged position he is led to occupy in certain situations, which is strictly speaking the following: that he is not the phallus. (S6, p. 350)

The subject feels he is deprived of something and the object fills in for that. We put *someone* in the place of what we feel we are missing. The object of human desire is "a decoy of being" which makes us feel we exist (see S6, p. 312, where Lacan equates the object with *Dasein*).

Fantasy

How does Lacan characterize our relationship to this other who incarnates or represents our lost jouissance? He calls it fantasy and formulates it as follows: ($\cancel{S} \lozenge a$).

Fantasy is thus, according to him, a certain relationship between the child, insofar as the child has become a divided subject—divided because he or she is alienated, castrated, missing something, deprived of something—and the little other as an object that somehow embodies what the child feels he or she has lost. Thus the fuller formula for fantasy, which we find implicitly at the end of "Subversion of the Subject" in *Écrits*, is:

$$\cancel{S} \lozenge \frac{a}{(-\varphi)}$$

I will fill out the notion of fantasy in Chap. 11. Let me simply note here that, regarding this little other, Lacan mentions "the essential role of identification with him," and sometimes refers to him as someone who is often "a brother who is barely older, or a friend his own age, [someone] who, in any case, has for him the prestige of being more virile and potent. The phallus appears here in its imaginary, not symbolic, form" (S5, p. 462).

We have now reviewed enough theory to turn to the dreams Lacan takes up in Seminar VI.

Part II

Analyzing Dreams

4

His Father had Died but Didn't Know It

This is not the first dream discussed in the Seminar, as the first is little Anna Freud's dream about strawberries. Rather it is the first *adult* dream Lacan takes up and, luckily enough, it is a very short dream, which at least on the face of it seems rather uncomplicated. He doesn't take it from the first edition of *The Interpretation of Dreams*, but from "Formulations on the Two Principles of Mental Functioning," published in 1911 (the dream was included in later editions of *The Interpretation of Dreams*).

A man, who had once nursed his father through a long and painful mortal illness, told me that in the months following his father's death he had repeatedly dreamt that ["]his father was alive once more and that he was talking to him in his usual way. But he felt it exceedingly painful that his father had really died, only without knowing it.["] The only way of understanding this apparently nonsensical dream is by adding "as the dreamer wished" or "as a result of his wish" after the words "that his father had really died," and by further adding "that he wished it" to the last words [thus: "only without knowing that his son wished it"]. The dream-thought then runs: it was a painful memory for him that he had been obliged to wish for his father's death (as a release) while [his father] was still alive, and how terrible it would have been if his father had had any suspicion of it! What

© The Author(s), under exclusive license to Springer Nature Switzerland AG 2025
B. Fink, *Lacan on Desire*, The Palgrave Lacan Series,
https://doi.org/10.1007/978-3-031-76386-1_4

we have here is thus the familiar case of self-reproaches after the loss of a loved one, and in this instance the self-reproach went back to the infantile significance of death-wishes against the father. [SE XII, p. 225]

Freud would thus have us read the dream as follows: The son felt it exceedingly painful that his father had died as a result of the son's death wish toward him. Yet the father didn't realize that his son had wished him dead.

Lacan finds Freud's account insufficient. Restoring these two censored clauses doesn't go far enough, he says (S6, p. 55). For it does not lay bare an unconscious wish in the dream other than the child's typically Oedipal wish for the father's death, which just so happens to converge with the adult's later wish for the father's death, albeit for different reasons: to put an end to the father's suffering.

Lacan sketches out a few things about the dream in the chapter of the Seminar in which it is presented, Chap. 3, and, as often happens in Lacan's Seminars, one arrives at a section in a class where many things he had begun to sketch out come together, or come to a head, as it were. I would suggest that this happens in Chap. 6, pages 96 to 102.

I shall try to summarize here what Lacan adds to Freud's discussion of the dream. He suggests that upon the death of a parent, specifically of one's father, one finds oneself next in line to die (S6, p. 96), next in line to be castrated ("it is [the son's] turn to be castrated," p. 92). In other words, one becomes preoccupied with the possibility of one's own death, after having witnessed the demise of one or more members of the previous generation. "We know that the death of one's father is always experienced as the disappearance of a sort of shield . . . with respect to the absolute master, death" (p. 116).

In my own experience, I have only heard this from one man, who was himself a psychoanalyst, and I have occasionally heard older friends of mine talk about feeling like they are next in line as the friends they had throughout their childhood and adulthood begin to disappear one after another. Lacan, nevertheless, seems to postulate this as something of a general phenomenon, and we might wonder if he himself was not a bit preoccupied with the question, knowing as we do that his father died in November 1960, less than two years after this discussion, while he was giving Seminar VIII. Lacan himself was pushing 60 and he even comments on his age in Seminar VI: "We, thank God, manage to forget that we are over 50, and we have reasons for doing so" (S6, p. 222). His father may have been declining or sick already at this time (this might go part of the way toward explaining the odd discussion of the "half-dead" at the end of Chap. 3; see pp. 58–9). So we might speculate that such a question was present for him in his own life. That is pure speculation, of course, for perhaps he heard it from a great many of his patients, colleagues, friends, and relatives.

Note that Lacan takes up quite a few dreams involving death, including another of Freud's examples, the well-known "father, can't you see I'm burning" dream (Seminar XVI, pp. 169–70), and a dream that Trotsky had also involving death (S6, p. 115). Interpreting a dream for Lacan often seems to involve situating the role of death in the dream and in the dreamer's life more generally. He goes so far as to claim that "what language always veils [is] death" (p. 23), and that every dream contains a death wish (p. 44)!

What does he tell us about this specific dream? He claims that "the precise desire in the dream [is] to stay ignorant" (S6, p. 96). To stay ignorant of what? To stay ignorant that one is next in line, that one will someday die perhaps just like the father did, a horribly painful death in which life went on long after the father's desire to live had disappeared. Lacan situates the desire to live as crucial to human beings and considers horrific the reduction of life to mere existence without desire—in other words, to the persistence of life despite the death of desire (p. 101).

Lacan reminds us that, during his father's illness, the dreamer was *well aware* that he wished his father would die because it would put the father out of his misery (we might speculate that he wished, too, to relieve himself of his own misery while caring for his father). That cannot, therefore, count as an unconscious desire.

And Lacan mentions the obvious notion, already mentioned by Freud, that the dreamer does not want to know that, as a child, he already wished his father dead, that wish not having come into being for the first time when his father was gravely ill. The child's Oedipal wish for the death of his father (and even for his castration as the child's rival; S6, p. 93) is the wish that is borrowed in the adult's dream, as Freud puts it here. (Freud even goes so far as to characterize the child's wish as the capitalist, and the adult's wish as the entrepreneur. The child provides the libidinal capital and the adult puts it to work.)

Lacan proposes that we see in this dream a desire to stay ignorant, *a desire not to know*. We are perhaps more familiar with the discussion of the desire for ignorance from Seminar XX (p. 1), but it is made quite explicit here already: the dreamer has a desire not to know at least two different things: (1) not to know that already, as a child, he had wished his father dead for reasons he would like to forget, (2) but also not to know that his number is up (next), so to speak.

Note that the subject's own willful ignorance is attributed to the father in the dream: it is the father who does not know something—in this case, that he is dead. It's as if the dreamer were asserting, "I'm not ignorant, you are." So there is a refusal to see his own will to ignorance, a wish not to see what he is up to, to see what he is unwilling to confront. Lacan calls this a "rejecting onto the other" or "casting onto the other" of the dreamer's own ignorance (S6, p. 96). *This desire not to know is the unconscious wish in the dream.*

Note that the pain the dreamer feels in the dream is displaced. In the dream it is supposedly generated by the father's ignorance of his own death, but the pain actually concerns what is coming for the dreamer: the possibility that he, too, may at some point end up outliving his desire to live. As Lacan puts it, we "count on" our desire and we are "afraid it will fail [us]" (S6, p. 101).

Insofar as the dream was presented to Freud as a recurrent dream that the patient had dreamt repeatedly for some time, Lacan suggests that the dreamer keeps attempting to interpose or erect the image of his father between himself and death. His father appears as an object, as a little other—not as the Other with a capital *O*, Lacan tells us, that is, *not* as an authority figure, an authoritative figure, or an ideal figure—but rather as an all-too-human body that is subject to illness and demise.

Lacan seems to suggest that, as children, we believe that the presence of our parent protects us from death. The image of the father is conjured up here to veil the dreamer's own impending death. And this image is repeatedly generated to remind the dreamer of his own desire to defeat his father, to know something his father didn't know, to castrate him—in short, it reminds the dreamer of one of his own important desires, desire being something that keeps death at bay, keeps the abyss of mere existence at bay (S6, p. 116).

Recall that at this stage in Lacan's work, little object *a* is nothing other than the little other—it is not yet the real cause of desire, as it becomes starting in Seminar VIII. By repeatedly invoking or picturing this little other in his dreams, the subject can hide and escape unscathed.

Lacan goes on to talk about how subjects very often flee or fade in the presence of the object. Indeed, he mentions cases of men who refuse to satisfy their sexual desires with a specific woman for fear that they will become dependent upon her for their satisfaction and thus fade away as subjects. "When he finds himself in the presence of object *a*, the subject vanishes" (S6, p. 102). He perhaps brings this up here because he senses that with his will not to know, our dreamer wishes to flee: he presents/ represents the object instead of himself. We will see a far clearer example of this when we turn, in Chap. 5, to the dream recounted by Ella Sharpe's patient.

Lacan also provides a discussion here of identification with the aggressor: the child identifies with his father, and having wanted the father dead, seems to have a death wish toward himself. In that sense, repeatedly picturing his father in dreams is designed to veil his "desire for [his own] death" (S6, p. 97). Freud might have said that a child or an adult might wish himself dead out of guilt for having wished others dead, but Lacan points to identification. Being just like his father, he too should die!

Lacan even goes so far as to say that a dream always contains two wishes: a desire to go on sleeping (as Freud said) and a death wish (S6, p. 44). Whether the death wish aims at another or oneself, or at oneself as another, is not made clear in that context.

Now why does a boy identify with his father? Because the father is thought to have successfully castrated, disarmed, or neutralized the mother, Lacan says (S6, p. 108). The father has transformed the mother from a praying mantis or devouring figure into a castrated being, into someone who is obviously lacking in certain respects, wanting in certain ways.

Lacan attempts to locate this dream on his Graph of Desire, so I will provide a quick, barebones sketch of it here. It will get filled out as we go along.

The Graph of Desire

The Graph (see Fig. 4.1) seems to grow out of a number of Lacan's explorations in mathematical fields like network theory (which, in mathematics, is part of "graph theory" and is used in electrical power systems; note that Lacan mentions "circuits" in Seminar VI), group theory (e.g., Klein groups), and cybernetics, traces of which can be found very clearly in the "Suite" to the "Seminar on 'The Purloined Letter'" in *Écrits* and in Seminar IV (class given on March 20, 1957).[1] The networks he provides in that "Suite" follow mathematical principles of transformation, and

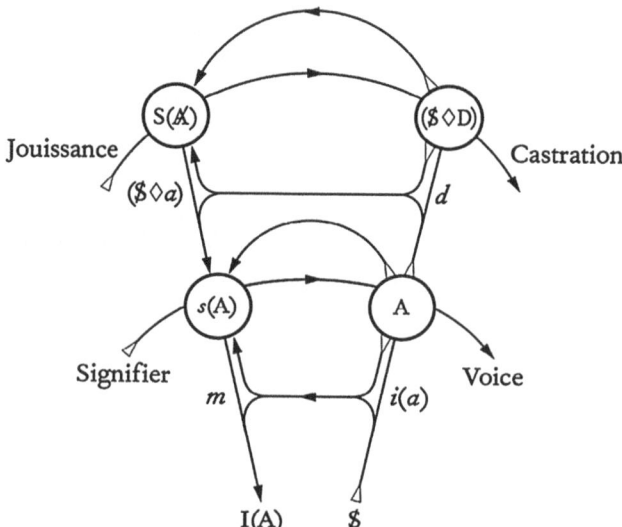

Fig. 4.1 Complete Graph of Desire (*Écrits*, p. 817)

---

[1] The parallelepiped that I included in Appendix 1 of *The Lacanian Subject* (Fink 1995) is included in that class in pirate versions, not the published version, although a related network can be found in the published French version on p. 232.

that was perhaps Lacan's goal for the nodes in the Graph of Desire, but I think the most we can claim here is that there are two sets of parallel lines between which he draws analogies (the main two horizontal lines, and then the two "in-between" lines).

I will describe the Graph diachronically to begin with, in other words, describing how it develops in time, over the course of time. But you should realize that Lacan also wants us to read it synchronically, as the relationship between the subject and the signifying system as a whole (S6, p. 367).

We begin in the lower righthand corner, where you see a sort of upward facing triangle, which Lacan sometimes dubs "intentionality." For our present purposes, let us initially call it *discomfort*. The infant experiences some sort of discomfort (triangle) and cries. The cry is heard by a caretaker (the Other, abbreviated as A for *Autre*), usually one of the parents, who has at his or her disposal a code by which to interpret that cry. He or she interprets the cry to mean one of a wide variety of possible things—for example, the baby is hungry, thirsty, overtired, has a wet diaper, feels lonely or left out, wants a hug, wants to be held, is being a pain in the neck, is just seeking attention, or what have you. The meaning attributed to the cry is found at $s(A)$, which is where we find the meaning attributed by the Other to the baby's cry (note that s, for signified [*signifié*] or meaning [*sens*], is in italics here, and thus imaginary).

This meaning can be said to be retroactively constituted insofar as the meaning was not there in the initial cry. Why is that? Because meaning is a product of language, and insofar as the baby did not express itself in words, it is the caregiver who retroactively attributes meaning to the baby's cry. It is retroactive insofar as the meaning is not at the origin of the cry, but rather created after the cry has already been heard and interpreted by someone else.

What this leads to, then, is an identification—at the point $I(A)$ on the Graph of Desire—of the baby as having a specific characteristic: you are hungry, you are greedy, you are lonely, you are a pain in the ass—the possibilities are endless! We might characterize this identification with words that Lacan uses in "The Mirror Stage": "Thou art that." Here we have the Other telling the child who he or she is.

This portion of the figure graphically portrays Lacan's oft-repeated thesis that meaning is determined in the place of the Other—in other words, that meaning is determined by the Other. Even when I feel I know what I mean, as a teacher, for example, or as an analysand on the couch, it is what my audience hears me say that determines its meaning. So regardless of our intention—and we can assume that little by little, a baby learns to distinguish a growling or gnawing sensation in the stomach from other sensations like that of having a wet diaper—the meaning will still be determined by other people, by the listener. Indeed, a parent can respond to every cry a baby makes with food, and end up convincing the child that it is always hungry, or at least that every discomfort can be dealt with by eating. Eating is the answer to whatever ails ya. Or it might be drinking.

Alternatively, a parent can respond to every cry a baby makes by yelling, and retroactively convince the child that it is fundamentally unwelcome in the world—indeed, a royal pain in the parent's ass. The child may conclude that it is best to shut up, or that getting a rise out of the parent is better than nothing. At the level of identification, the message conveyed to the child may be that it is a punching bag, that it is the source of all of the parent's misery in life, that it should never have been born, or some combination of those things: "Thou art worthless," "Thou art a piece of shit." And, indeed, certain of our analysands report hearing declarations of this kind in their heads quite frequently!

Now what happens as the child begins to learn to speak, and to put its discomfort into words? The Other remains all-powerful here, continuing to have the ability to "hear" everything the child says in ways the child clearly did not intend, transforming (some might say "twisting") the meaning of the child's demands (recall that a demand is a need or discomfort put into words) however the Other likes. They could be interpreted one way one day, and another the next day. Or they could always be interpreted in the same way: even though the child is asking to be held, the bottle may be shoved in its mouth and the child ignored.

Yet, even when the Other is someone of relatively good faith, who makes a concerted effort to understand what the child is intending to request, and to satisfy it, there is always a leftover, a remainder—the kind we discussed earlier. And, as I said earlier, *it is that very leftover, that very thing which is not and structurally cannot be expressed in my request, that constitutes desire*, according to Lacan. It is the remainder of my experience of need that fails to be fully expressed in words and that persists after my demand is formulated, and even after I have been given what I explicitly asked for.

This takes us toward the upper floor or stage of the Graph, specifically to the intermediate stage where we see *d* for desire on the righthand side. The upper part of the Graph is where what Lacan calls the "drama of desire" is played out, the drama of unconscious desire. (We will return to this in Part III when we discuss *Hamlet*.)

Now, regarding how Lacan locates the dream about the dead father on the Graph of Desire, note that he initially puts "He is dead" on the lower horizontal line, where the statement (the "process [or: unfolding] of the statement"; S6, p. 71) is situated. The upper line is that of enunciation ("the enunciation process"; p. 72). However, a bit further on (pp. 88–9), we see that he situates "He was dead" on the line of enunciation; it is something, after all, that only speaking beings can say (animals may observe that a fellow animal is no longer moving or breathing, but cannot formulate something like "she is dead" and communicate it to others; Lacan says, "'he was dead' means absolutely nothing to a being who does not speak"). He locates the words "He did not know" on the lower line. He seems to refer to the latter as "the unsaid," which is obviously related to the unconscious. It is also related to the wish not to know (p. 97): not to know he wished his father dead (and the wish that his father not know that either?).

But then on pp. 113–4 (see Fig. 4.2), they are again inverted: "He did not know" is on the upper line. (This is where he locates it much later, too; see S16, p. 237.) So go figure as to the importance of the Graph of Desire in helping us situate dreams! Lacan does use the Graph on a few further occasions: on page 133 he situates the dream text on the horizontal lower line and the recounting of the dream on the upper line (to the left), suggesting that analytic enunciation (or free association) is located there too.

At the end of Seminar V, the Seminar in which the Graph is first introduced, Lacan says that the upper line is "a sort of sentence that the subject cannot articulate, and that we have to help him articulate, which structures the whole of his neurosis" (S5, p. 449).

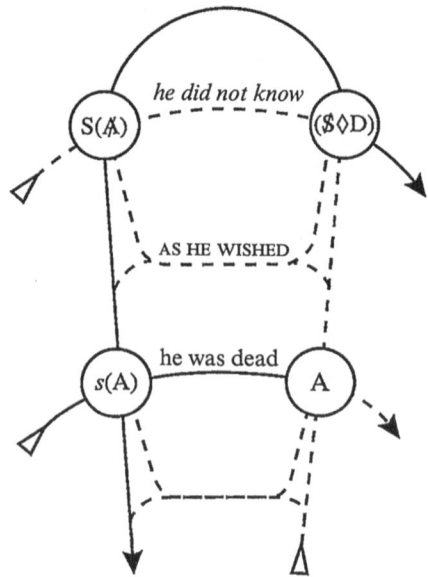

Fig. 4.2 Dream text on the Graph of Desire (S6, p. 114)

All of the neurotic's behavior presents itself as speech, and even as full speech [...] but it is entirely cryptic, unknown to the subject as regards its meaning, even though he pronounces it with all of his being, by everything he manifests, by everything he evokes and ineluctably brings about in a certain path of achievement and non-achievement, unless something intervenes which involves the kind of oscillation known as psychoanalysis. It is speech, pronounced by the barred subject, barred from himself, that we call the unconscious. (S5, p. 450)

The upper line is dotted to indicate the fragmentation of analytic enunciation—the way in which hesitation and doubt, selective stress and glossing over of terms, appear in the analysand's speech, and are underscored by the analyst. This leads to what Lacan here calls the "fragmentation" (S6, p. 139) of the text, the "detaching" of signifiers from one another and breaking them down even as far as single phonemes. Lacan says: "we make the current signification vacillate in order to allow the signifiers that are involved in the enunciation to become detached from each other" (p. 140).

Freud might have called this encouraging free association to each of the "elements" of the dream. He wrote:

We should disregard the apparent coherence between a dream's elements as an unessential illusion, and trace back the origin of each of its elements on its own account. (SE V, p. 449)

To take up an example of a signifier that is never associated to in the course of the long discussion of the dream recounted by Ella Sharpe's patient, to which we will turn next, consider the signifier *Czechoslovakia*. Apart from simply reiterating it to the patient or asking obvious questions—like "Have you ever been there?" or "What have you heard about it?"—what might we do with it?

We might accentuate it differently or slowly: CZECHoslovakia. Or proffer check oh slow vakia; check in the mail/male; checkmate; vacate; vacation; so slow. If the dreamer also speaks French, we could reiterate *vaquer* (to do or go about [one's business]). If he speaks Spanish or Italian, we could enunciate *vaca* or *vacca* (cow). In this way, we break down part of the dream text into smaller and smaller elements and encourage the analysand to associate to them.

Lacan puts the Graph to further use in Seminar VI when he comments on page 158 that the question the patient raises about the little cough he gives before entering Sharpe's office—"What kind of message could it be?"—can be situated along the hook at the top of the Graph. The patient's question seems to be "What do I mean by coughing uncontrollably like that?" And as Lacan puts it, "he literally raises a question concerning the Other that is in him—namely, his unconscious" (S6, p. 159).

Further on, he draws on the Graph something that he refers to as the circuit of free association (p. 168), which leads the subject to $S(\cancel{A})$. It seems that we are to understand here that free association loops around between desire, fantasy, the drive, and the signifier of the lack in the Other.

Lacan tells us that the purpose of his topological models like the Graph is to put into a more methodical structure Freud's first and second topographies, for example (S6, p. 239), which are often used in highly confusing and self-contradictory ways. "Did he succeed?" I'll return to the question further on.

Excursus on Free Association

I will illustrate free association, which purportedly occurs in the upper circuit of the Graph, with a clinical example, one in which an analysand of mine professed to be unable to decide if a certain color in a dream was blue or green. Following Freud, *I took the indecision itself to be particularly significant*, as if the dream thoughts behind that portion of the dream were so laden with unpalatable memories and/or meanings that, even in the remembering of the dream, some subterfuge had to be engaged in to throw the now-awake dreamer off the scent, introducing some disturbance in the enunciation of the dream ("uh. . . uh. . . I'm not sure"). I refused to be distracted by the analysand's doubt as to whether it was blue or green and took both alternatives extremely seriously, asking for associations to both terms (cf. SE IV, pp. 317–8).

This analysand ended up recalling a very powerful scene from his past (a scene he professed not to have thought about in a very long time, perhaps not since it occurred some twenty-five years earlier) simply by associating to the color of an object that appeared in a dream he had had about selecting a notebook in a shop. The analysand felt he was correcting the former description ("blue") with the latter ("green"), but eventually concluded that the color of the object in the dream was the same as that of the "powder blue" carpet in his dining room growing up. At that point, he suddenly recalled that one day he had been lying on that carpet and had heard sounds coming from the next room; he had gotten up and looked through the louvered doors between the dining room and the family room where he glimpsed his mother and brother having sex on the floor, their bodies being visually cut into odd horizontal slices by the louvers.

Having recollected this scene thanks to our associative work on the dream, the disturbing images he had been having around that time of partial bodies engaging in sexual acts tapered off. The scene alluded to by this dream element ("blue or green") could hardly have been guessed at from the manifest content of the dream (which initially seemed almost as boring as Freud's dream of "the botanical monograph"; SE IV, pp. 169–73, 282–4); nevertheless, this early childhood scene seems to have been one of the latent thoughts that went into the construction of the dream. Had

I taken the bait and allowed myself to be dissuaded from inquiring into the color owing to its supposed uncertainty, this memory might have taken much longer to come to light and the distressing images that came with it might have persisted for quite some time.[2]

What Is an Association?

As odd as it may seem, what constitutes an "association" is not always crystal clear to analysands or even to analysts who are just beginning to practice. Nor does it always seem transparently obvious to analysts *how* to encourage analysands to free associate. Which is why I'd like to comment on it briefly here.

How, for example, might we encourage a relatively inexperienced analysand to associate to the word "blue"? We might simply query, "Blue?" or "What about blue?" or even "What comes to mind about blue?" Faced with a shrug of the shoulders or the banal response, "The sky is blue," we might ask whether it seemed to be a particular shade of blue and, if so, can the dreamer describe it. The words with which he then describes it may lead off in a useful direction, but if he is unable to give any details about it, we might then ask whether he recalls ever having seen that particular shade of blue anywhere.

Should the attempt to encourage the dreamer to associate to the *color* blue go nowhere, there are other equally important avenues to explore, for the word "blue" may also imply melancholy, gloom, or mild depression—in other words, it is a signifier with several different signifieds, and may serve as what Freud calls a "switch-word" or "verbal bridge" from a visual image to an idea, or from one idea (usually a somewhat simple one) to another (SE V, p. 341 n. 1; SE VII, pp. 65 n, 82, and 90; SE X, p. 213). "Blue" may also designate a team (the blue team, for example, as opposed to the red team); it is part of expressions like "black and blue," "out of the blue," "the wild blue yonder," and "the deep blue sea"; it may make one think of "the blues," whether in reference to a musical tradition, a mood, or an army during a particular war (or even of bands like

---

[2] For a fuller account of this case, see Chapter 11 in Fink (2014b).

The Moody Blues or The Blues Brothers), or of bluebells (a type of flower), Blue Bonnet (a butter substitute), baby blue (which may allude to the topic of having children), sky blue, "Little Boy Blue" (a nursery rhyme), or blue balls (a painful male condition)—the list goes on and on. Depending on the analysand, any of these could prove to be extremely useful associations, reminding the analysand, for example, of events of the previous day, weeks, or years, previously unmentioned times in his life, or long-forgotten sexual experiences.

There is no way for the analyst to know in advance whether a particular way of associating to signifiers will be of use in someone's analysis; we can, however, gauge whether a particular way of associating turns out to be useful over the course of time in a specific analysand's work. One analysand may fruitfully dwell on homonyms like "blew." Another on the letters contained within the signifier, "blue" making him think, for example, of "lube" and "lube job" in English; recall that Wolfgang Mozart signed his letters to his sister with a variety of anagrams of his own name, most often Gnagflow Trazom (see Freud's comments on "the analysis and synthesis of syllables," SE IV, p. 297 n). But another analysand may play around with the letters in a word and never alight upon anything that seems germane either to the dream or to his life experience. An old-fashioned poet (or a fan of Cockney rhyming slang) may usefully think, in connection with "blue," of slough, slew, brew, flu, stew, chew, hew, or loo, because that is how his mind works in general, whereas for most others such rhyming associations will lead nowhere. One analysand may be productively reminded of the stressful time when he wore blue in the Navy; another may recount a number of occasions on which he wore blue clothing to work in recent weeks, none of which seem to ever connect up with the dream itself.

Some analysands seem to take the invitation to "free associate" as license to move further and further away from the dream in a kind of infinite "stream of consciousness." The analyst must thus not lose sight of the fact that the goal of association is to elucidate the backdrop of the dream, and must put a stop to seemingly fruitless trains of thought by calling the analysand back to some other portion or element of the dream to see if something more productive will arise from associating to other signifiers in it.

5

The Dream Recounted by Ella Sharpe's Patient

In Seminar VI, Lacan briefly discusses a second dream dreamt by an adult: the one dreamt by Trotsky in which Lenin appears. It brings up many of the same themes as the dream about the father who did not know he was dead, so we will leave it aside here and turn directly to the far more elaborate dream recounted by Ella Sharpe's patient. We will not exhaustively cover all the associations to it that the analyst is able to elicit from her patient, all of her comments on it, and all of Lacan's comments on her comments. Instead, I will cite the text of the dream and then examine Lacan's interpretation of it. The dream itself must be reconstructed a bit, as it came out of the patient's mouth interspersed with incidental comments and associations (I have included them in brackets), as dreams often do. Here is more or less what Sharpe managed to record:

> I dreamt I was taking a journey with my wife around the world, and we arrived in Czechoslovakia where all kinds of things were happening. I met a woman on a road, a road that now reminds me of the road I described to you in the two other dreams lately in which I was having sexual play with a woman in front of another woman. So it happened in this dream. This

© The Author(s), under exclusive license to Springer Nature Switzerland AG 2025
B. Fink, *Lacan on Desire*, The Palgrave Lacan Series,
https://doi.org/10.1007/978-3-031-76386-1_5

time my wife was there while the sexual event occurred. The woman I met was very passionate looking [*and I am reminded of a woman I saw in a restaurant yesterday. She was dark and had very full lips, very red and passionate looking, and it was obvious that had I given her any encouragement she would have responded. She must have stimulated the dream, I expect.*] In the dream the woman wanted intercourse with me and she took the initiative [*which as you know is a course which helps me a great deal. If the woman will do this I am greatly helped*]. In the dream the woman actually lay on top of me; that has only just come to my mind. She was evidently intending to put my penis in her body. I could tell that by the maneuvers she was making. I disagreed with this, but she was so disappointed I thought that I would masturbate her. (Sharpe 1937, p. 132; cited in S6, pp. 143–4)

The patient then editorializes: "It sounds quite wrong to use that verb transitively. One can say 'I masturbated' and that is correct, but it is all wrong to use the word transitively" (Sharpe 1937, p. 133).[1] Later he adds a few more details to his account of the dream:

There was no orgasm. I remember her vagina gripped my finger. I see the front of her genitals, the end of the vulva. Something large and projecting hung downwards like a fold on a hood. Hoodlike it was, and it was this that the woman made use of in maneuvering to get my penis. The vagina seemed to close round my finger. The hood seemed strange. (Sharpe 1937, p. 133)

Lacan considers two things to be of great import here: the moment at which the dream comes to the patient's mind in the course of the session, and his editorializing remark about the transitive use of the verb "masturbate." He goes at great length through everything Sharpe recorded about what transpired in the session prior to the patient's recounting of the dream, taking things up in order.

The patient thinks of the dream after discussing the "little cough" he began making just before opening the door to his analyst's consulting room the last few times he came to see her. "Why would I cough?" he wonders. To announce himself, as he used to do (around age 15) with his

---

[1] In our times, he might have been less struck by the transitive use of the word.

older brother, when his brother would be with his girlfriend in a room that the patient wanted to enter, presumably because he hoped to spare them the embarrassment of being caught kissing. What might the analyst be doing in her office that he would have to spare her the embarrassment of being caught red-handed doing? Masturbating, no doubt. For, he comments, he would not have been invited to go up to her office (by her housemaid or secretary, in all likelihood) if there were another person in the office with her.

Masturbation reminds him of a dog that he once allowed to masturbate on his leg, even though someone might have come into the room where it was occurring. It is at this point in his thoughts about masturbation, and the analyst's imagined masturbation, that the patient coughs again and says the following: " I do not know why I should now think of my dream last night" (Sharpe 1937, p. 132).[2]

Lacan emphasizes that the patient cannot bear to think of his analyst as someone who is less than ideal or perfect, certainly not as someone who might be sitting in her office masturbating between two patients! Recall the patient's response to Sharpe's question: "Why cough before coming in here?" He replies, "That is absurd, because naturally I should not be asked to come up if someone were here, and I do not think of you in that way at all" (Sharpe 1937, p. 131).

He does not think of her in that way at all! He can't possibly allow himself to imagine her doing anything sexual, whether alone or with someone else. She has to be maintained as some kind of an ideal figure or absolute Other with a capital *O* for him. As we shall see, this is crucial to Lacan's interpretation of the dream.

I myself have had a number of analysands who mentioned to me that they imagined I was touching myself during a session or had just had intercourse before a session, fantasies that had specific meanings for each of them. But this particular patient feels he has to thrust such an idea

---

[2] At one point in his commentary (p. 170), Lacan mistakenly says that it was at this point that the patient first remembered the dream, but, as you can see, the text is vaguer, suggesting rather that it was at this point in the session that he first thought of recounting it to his analyst: "I do not know why I should now think of my dream last night" (p. 132). Given how methodical the patient is, according to Sharpe, everything he says having been carefully thought out, it is hard to imagine he hadn't planned on talking about the dream before coming to his session that day.

aside, even though it obviously came to his mind. His analyst is not allowed to represent anything less than perfection and perhaps even virginity to him. In short, she is a sort of Madonna figure here.

Let us note that Sharpe herself concluded that, because the patient thought of the dream right after talking about masturbation, the dream must, therefore, be a masturbation fantasy (Sharpe 1937, p. 138). Lacan does not immediately disagree with her about this, but he turns things around. Recall the patient's comment that, since the passionate-looking woman in the dream "was so disappointed [that I would not have intercourse with her], I thought that I would masturbate her" (p. 133). Lacan highlights the patient's editorialization: "It sounds quite wrong to use that verb transitively. One can say 'I masturbated' and that is correct, but it is all wrong to use the word transitively" (p. 133).

Lacan immediately concludes that the patient's real thought is, if the woman who is trying to have sex with me isn't happy, let her go masturbate—that is, she can just do it herself, take care of herself, get off by herself. He is not going to participate. He is not only going to keep his penis out of the game, he is even going to keep his finger out of the game.

Lacan goes so far as to liken what he does with this dream to what Freud did with the dream of the father who did not know he was dead: Lacan suggests that he is interpreting the dream "by restoring the avoided signifiers" (S6, p. 155). The avoided signifiers in this case are "she can just go masturbate by herself" and leave me alone (presumably).[3]

Fantasy

Lacan juxtaposes, and indeed compares and contrasts, fantasies and dreams here. He mentions the patient's fantasy as a boy of being in a room that he was not supposed to be in, and imagining barking like a dog so no one would come in looking for him, telling themselves instead, "Oh, it's only a dog in there." Curiously enough, Sharpe never tells us what room he was in, why he was not supposed to be there, and what he

---

[3] On page 159, Lacan comments that "he does not want her to take care of him," and raises the question why, but I don't believe he ever comes back to this question.

might possibly have been doing in it, all of which seem to me to be quite relevant—but such is life.

Lacan proposes here that *fantasy emphasizes the subject*, not the object (S6, p. 175), whereas a *dream emphasizes the object*, not the subject (S6, p. 176).[4] And he characterizes the object here as "the object involved in desire." It is not clear what use he intends to make of this distinction, but we can try to reconstruct that in the fantasy, the child is imagining getting some kind of illicit pleasure from being in a place where he is not supposed to be and getting away with it, because he dupes people into thinking he is not there. Insofar as he imagines playing the part of a dog in that fantasy scenario by barking, we might imagine that he was engaging in some kind of masturbatory activity of his own (not unlike the dog's?), and perhaps looking at pictures in that room, but we are left to our own projections here.

To the degree to which this fantasy emphasizes the subject, it is a subject who is not who he claims to be or passes himself off as: a dog. It is a subject who is invisible to others ("hiding in plain sight"). As in Poe's story of *The Purloined Letter*, something precious is disguised as a worthless scrap of paper. The subject is someone who is having a good time under everybody's noses, procuring some kind of enjoyment for himself while duping everyone else. The Other here is dupable, credulous, certainly not all-knowing. And the subject is slippery, the invisible man. "He makes himself into something other than what he is" (S6, p. 163). "The patient is never where we expect him to be, he slips from one point to another" (p. 195). "The goal of his fantasy—its meaning or obvious content—is to show that he is not where he is" (p. 161). "The subject appears elided" in his fantasy of barking like a dog (p. 167); he is not there but is replaced by an imaginary other, the dog.[5]

Yet, just as Freud says regarding dreams, Lacan suggests here that "the subject identifies with all the parties to the fantasy" (S6, p. 174). We have to wonder if he considers this to be a general principle, because earlier he

---

[4] Later in the Seminar, he seems to associate neurosis with an emphasis on the barred subject in fantasy and perversion with an emphasis on the object in fantasy (S6, p. 314).

[5] Regarding the patient discussed in "Direction of the Treatment," Lacan opines, "His being is always elsewhere. He has 'tucked it away,' one might say. Am I saying this to explain the difficulty of his desire? No, rather to say that his desire is for difficulty" (*Écrits*, p. 529).

had said that people who have the fantasy that "a child is being beaten" identify with the instrument used during the beating. Perhaps he means they primarily identify with it, and only secondarily with the other two or three parties to the fantasy (after all, they identify with the rival child being beaten and with the aggressor doing the beating, too).

In what way, then, is the object emphasized in dreams? Recall here, once again, that the object is not the object as cause of the subject's desire at this stage in Lacan's work. Rather, it is the little other like oneself. Where do we see such a little other in the dream recounted by Ella Sharpe's patient? Is it the woman who wants to have sex with him? Is it his wife who, as he tells us, was silently witnessing the scene? This is far from clear at first.

On page 176, Lacan proposes that the object foregrounded in the dream is the passionate-looking woman.[6] It seems to me that what allows Lacan to say that "masturbating the other and the patient masturbating [are] one and the same thing" (S6, p. 198) is that he sees the patient and the passionate-looking woman as a and a' on the L Schema (Fig. 5.1) (or as m and $i(a)$ on the lower level of the Graph of Desire).

Lacan in fact provides a series of little others for this patient: his sister, the dog, and the couple (consisting of his brother and the brother's girlfriend).[7] Note, too, that Lacan says that this patient has for a long time been "propped up by his identification with a woman," and there he is talking about the patient's sister (S6, p. 224). "His sister is clearly $i(a)$ for him" (p. 223).

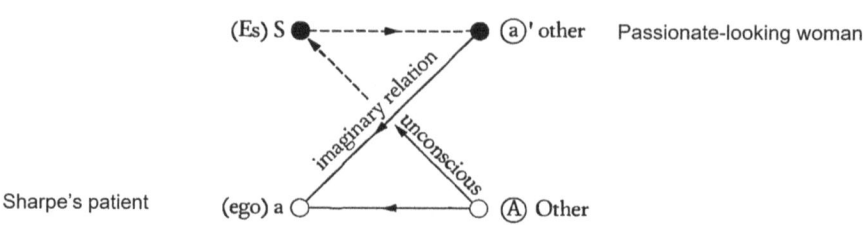

Fig. 5.1 The L Schema (*Écrits*, p. 40)

---

[6] On page 181, it seems to be the image of her hooded vagina.

[7] Other possible candidates for $i(a)$ are his female friend who does impersonations and the guy who offered to get him hood material for his golf bag.

The Places of the subject, the little other (or object), and the Other with a capital *O*

Now according to Lacan, in analyzing dreams, as in analyzing any psychoanalytic "phenomenon," we always have to indicate "the places of the subject, the little other [or object], and the Other with a capital *O*" (S6, p. 193). I'm not sure he actually spells out who or what occupies each of those places in this specific dream, but what he says about the subject is that he is never where you think he is or where he appears to be. In Sharpe's terms: "His great aim is not to betray himself and to control anything that gives him away" (Sharpe 1937, p. 130).

Consider the analogy that Sharpe provides of analysis with this patient as like a game of chess. Where is the subject (S6, p. 195)? Even at the end of the game when there are only a few pieces left on the board, can we say that he is the king, the rook, the bishop, or the pawn (p. 203)? No, he is somehow ever-shifting and never definitively found in any piece. This is something we find in many cases of obsession: the subject is never willing to be pinned down, or considered to be this or that, but always has to be a plethora of things, has to occupy myriad positions, and can never allow himself to be considered to be one single thing. He is always more than people think he is or seem to want to say he is. He never truly throws his hat into the ring of any one specific activity, never puts it all on the line in any one particular endeavor, never bets all of his chips on any one venture (or partner), always needing to have several different irons in the fire, so to speak.

He can't be learning but one language at a time, but has to study two or three simultaneously. He doesn't read one theoretical text at a time, but rather five or six. He isn't just a waiter in a restaurant, but is also an actor, a musician, a day trader in stocks, and is writing a screenplay and designing a new video game. He cannot embrace one particular philosophy, religion, or approach to psychoanalysis, but has to forge his own. As a musician, no genre of music is big enough to contain his genius.

Contemporary approaches to psychology tax such people with grandiosity, and the man in the street considers them to be narcissistic or full of themselves. But what we see as psychoanalysts is that they are subjects grappling with castration, with giving something up. Creative musicians often combine genres, and invent new genres, but they have usually spent a great deal of time learning and assimilating one genre thoroughly first, only then moving on to assimilate others as well, and doing whatever they like with those. In the case of obsessives, what we tend to find, instead, is the old expression: "jack of all trades, master of none." They refuse to buckle down and focus, fearing that it would be too self-limiting.

The subject in the dream is the one who is the object of everyone's attention: the passionate-looking woman wants to have sex with him, and his wife is watching. But when it comes to his own participation in the action, he "craps out," as we say; he isn't there for anyone, he escapes, disappears. The obsessive is never "where he seems to designate himself at any particular moment in time" (S8, p. 297).

As for the Other with a capital O, it might appear to be his wife here, who is the silent witness to the scene—she sees all. Or we might consider the Other with a capital O to be Sharpe to whom the dream is recounted, for its meaning is going to arise in the place of the Other with a capital O. Sharpe herself is not explicitly present in the dream, but we might say that insofar as the patient has been in analysis with her for some time, she is implicitly present, in the sense that we can view dreams that are dreamt in the course of an analysis as dreamt for the analyst, as dreamt in order to be told to the analyst, as playing "a role in the ongoing analytic dialogue" (S6, p. 142). As Lacan puts it, "Briefly stated, dreams are dreamt not only for the analysis but often for the analyst, and they bear a message within the analysis" (p. 142).

As for the place of the object or little other, we began to broach it earlier. Based on what Lacan tells us about obsession in Seminar IV and in "Direction of the Treatment," I would hypothesize that it is the passionate-looking woman in the dream who is the little other for him, and that he organizes "circus games," as Lacan calls them, between himself as an ego (as a) and her (as a') to provide some sort of entertainment for the Other with a capital O: his wife and his analyst (see Fig. 5.2).

Note, furthermore, that the woman in the dream has dark hair, and that his mother did too. That could make her his alter ego (S6, p. 141). Like his mother, who used to pin him into his pram (or bed?), she is

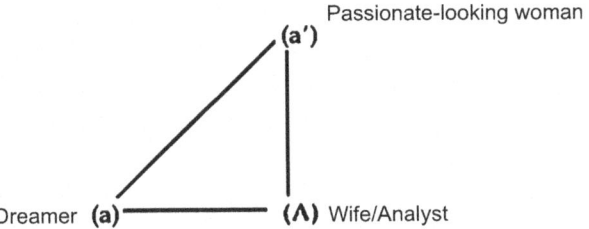

Fig. 5.2 Truncated L Schema

"pinning him down" in the dream—lying on top of him. And insofar as he hates seeing children constrained in any way, strapped into anything, like prams, his cutting up of the straps of his sister's sandals (which were like those of prams) may suggest an identification with his sister—she who perhaps also had dark hair like her mother.

Lacan points out an identification between the patient and his sister, for the patient says that his memory does not really begin until age 11, which was precisely how old his sister was when their father died. Lacan often indicates that to be an alter ego whose image is taken into one's own image of oneself, the other child—the semblable—has to be very close in age to oneself (see, for example, S6, p. 216). This would seem to rule out his sister as a little other for him (for she is eight years older than him), and yet Lacan himself points to an identification there: "It seems that this must have some connection with the fact that he is imaginarily alienated in his sister. His sister is clearly *i(a)* for him" (p. 223).

Such a hypothesis would then allow us to point out the curious fact that the hood in the dream—which is mentioned in close proximity to a song about hats and "tiles" (or top hats)—is never considered to be a possible representation of a foreskin or condom! If the patient is the ego and the passionate-looking woman is ego′, she may be presented in the dream as like him, as some kind of mirror image of him—that is, as having a penis too. (Sharpe [1937, p. 144] does at one point equate the "projection" of the hood with a penis, but not Lacan.)

Note, too, that the patient admits he once masturbated someone else (as incorrect as the transitive use seems to him to be): a boy his own age (Sharpe 1937, p. 133). Given all the associations around the hood to redness, lips, and labia, this might suggest an early confusion on his part about the exact nature of female genitalia (intersecting Sharpe's comments about the vagina dentata; cf. the limerick).[8] Lacan does mention "an ambiguous character related to a certain way of apprehending sexual relations" and introduces the phrase "psychical circumcision" (S6, p. 189).

We might have thought that his brother would be a better candidate for being his semblable, but we are never told how old he is (he might be only two years older than him or ten). All we know is that the patient thought about separating his brother from his brother's girlfriend, just like the patient, perhaps, thought about separating his mother and his father as a very young child by wetting his bed or having colic—so says Sharpe, at any rate, for whom bedwetting is a compulsive aggressive act of childhood designed to separate parents, to stop them from having sex. She postulates that her patient had "aggressive rival phantasies towards [his father] that in infancy were expressed in bodily ways"—colic, flatulence, and bedwetting (Sharpe 1937, p. 147). For Lacan, on the other hand, bedwetting is the result of excitement during parental intercourse (S6, pp. 190 and 208).

"Where Is the Subject?"

Where, then, is the subject—as opposed to the ego—located on the L schema? Nowhere, for the schema is truncated, just as it is in the case of the obsessive that Lacan describes in "Direction of the Treatment" (*Écrits*, p. 527).

Why is it, we might ask, that the obsessive subject can't be located? The easy answer is that, since his desire is the Other's desire, and since he feels the need to cancel out the Other's desire in order to exist, his desire, too, is canceled out and cannot come to the fore.

---

[8] There was a young lady from China
   Who mistook for her mouth her vagina.
   Her clitoris huge
   She covered with rouge,
   And lipsticked her labia minor.

Another possibility, which is not mentioned by Lacan, is that, since he never knows in advance which activity will make him the phallus again, get him the kind of attention that he wants in order to feel like he *is* the phallus, he has to try everything, every possible avenue, and that requires him to try nothing exclusively.

Now, just as his subject position can't be found, because it keeps shifting, so does his object. As we see in Seminar VIII (S8, p. 250), there is a constant metonymic slippage of objects in his desire from a to a', to a'', a''', etc. (cf. S6, p. 360), all of those *a*s being equated with the imaginary phallus:

$$\cancel{A} \; \lozenge \; \varphi \left(a, \, a', \, a'', \, a''', \, \ldots \right)$$

I won't go into the complications of the formula for his fantasy here, but we clearly see the serialization of objects in the parentheses, which can all play the same role for him insofar as their relation to the imaginary phallus is the same.

"Where Is the Phallus?"

When interpreting dreams, Lacan almost always seems to raise the question "Where is the phallus?" (S6, pp. 202 and 204–5). He does so in "Direction of the Treatment" (given as a talk in July 1958, about six months before he discussed Ella Sharpe's case) as well when discussing a male patient of his (*Écrits*, p. 527).[9]

---

[9] Lacan's patient was a man of mature years who

was impotent with his mistress and, having gotten it into his head to use his discoveries about the function of the potential third party in the couple, he suggested that she sleep with another man to see. [...]

It will come as no surprise that, without wasting any time—indeed, that very night—she had a dream, which she recounted to our crestfallen patient hot off the presses.

In the dream she had a phallus—she sensed its shape under her clothing—which did not prevent her from having a vagina as well, nor, especially, from wanting this phallus to enter it.

On hearing this, my patient's powers were immediately restored and he demonstrated this brilliantly to his shrewd paramour. (p. 527)

Recall what Lacan said about the phallus earlier: "The subject both is and is not the phallus" (S6, p. 214). The child is, at the outset, a precious phallic object for its mother, he suggests, but he then learns that a great deal is expected of him: he must learn to speak, become toilet trained, learn manners, etc. Hence, he is no longer the phallus. "Language and the law of language take [his position as the phallus] away from him" (p. 214).

No longer *being* the phallus (for his mother), he can finally *have* the phallus in a certain sense, he can wield it. Yet in the case of Sharpe's patient, Lacan seems to suggest that the patient is unable to wield the phallus. Instead, he tucks it off to the side in the form of his wife, who sits on the sidelines, looking on. Insofar as she is his precious object, or she is him insofar as he would like to still be the precious object for his mother, she cannot be put at risk by joining in the action. The wife qua phallus, like the analyst qua Other or Madonna, has to remain above the fray.

In the dream we have a representation of the imaginary or so-called *maternal phallus* in the form of the exaggeratedly long hood in the dream; hence the presence of a penis-like structure instead of an absence, instead of lack. This patient is going to be damned-well sure not to encounter the lack in the Other!

Lacan declares in this context that "The fundamental mainspring of neurosis is not to want the Other to be castrated" (S6, p. 229). He had already declared this in "Direction of the Treatment": "the refusal of castration, if there is any such thing, is first and foremost a refusal of the Other's castration (of the mother's, first of all)" (*Écrits*, p. 528). Regarding Sharpe's patient, he says, "The subject is [...] far from being able to recognize that the Other is castrated, but no further than he is from being able to recognize that he himself is" (S6, p. 159).

How, thus, does Lacan locate the phallus in this dream? It is not absent. It is located in the Other, who is, in this case, his wife. Woman as Other is whole, not castrated.

Lacan claims in "Direction of the Treatment" that he is not analyzing the mistress' dream but merely its effect on his patient, but there is clearly some analysis of the dream that takes place on the couple of pages devoted to it, which are quite relevant to our discussion of the dream dreamt by Sharpe's patient.

Not wanting the Other to be castrated is just as germane in hysteria. Lacan regularly talks about the hysteric as propping up the father—usually a father who is perceived by the hysteric to be weak in one or more essential ways. She tends to use herself to plug up the lack or failings in the father. (In Chap. 3, I mentioned a female patient of mine who terribly resented her younger brother; she also signed her life away to try to prevent her father from going bankrupt.)

When we consider the series of $i(a)$s (his sister, the dog, and the couple), the candidates for the Other and/or phallus (wife and analyst), and where the subject is located (everywhere and nowhere), we might wonder if Lacan's mathemes have really helped us simplify things compared to Freud's two topographies (conscious, preconscious, unconscious, and id, ego, superego). Consider what Lacan says about the latter:

> We try here to develop guides that allow us to resituate the different organs of the mental apparatus, which Freud gave us in the successive stages of his thought, in a way that takes into account the fact that they only partially overlap, semantically speaking.
>
> It is not by putting them all together into one big set that we can make them function properly. We can do so, as it were, only by situating them in a framework that we attempt to make more fundamental, in such a way that we know what we are doing with all of these references when we work with them. (S6, p. 239).

Did Lacan succeed? Whether or not we ultimately conclude that he managed to provide something more methodical or fundamental than Freud's topographies, we can, in any case, see here an attempt to use models derived from network theory to provide a surer foundation for psychoanalysis. It is part of Lacan's broader attempt to mathematize psychoanalysis, to place psychoanalysis on a mathematical footing.

What Is the Unconscious Desire Expressed/ Satisfied in the Dream?

Having attempted to lay out how Lacan situates the subject, the little other, and the phallus in the dream, we must finally ask: What, then, is the unconscious desire expressed, if not satisfied, in the dream? In "Direction of the Treatment" Lacan tells us that "unconscious desire is the Other's desire" (*Écrits*, p. 528). What is the Other's desire in the dream? Something for us to ponder!

Think of the young homosexual woman's dreams (SE XVIII, pp. 147–72) that included themes of marriage: she took marriage to be her parents' desire for her, and Freud's too. Freud ended up concluding that her dreams thus staged desires that were other people's, not her own. His fellow analysts found that a shocking idea. Dreams, they felt, had to fulfill the dreamer's own deepest wishes, not other people's wishes!

Let us consider the possibility that the wish satisfied in the dream is the Other's wish. And let us provisionally take the Other here to be Ella Sharpe herself. The patient has undoubtedly come to realize, over the course of time, that she wants him to confess that he has rivalrous and aggressive tendencies, something he does not seem to believe. In the dream, it is the little other—that is the passionate-looking woman—who takes the initiative and might be characterized as somewhat aggressively trying to do something—namely, "get [his] penis" (Sharpe 1937, p. 133). Rather than seeming to confirm Sharpe's desire, the dream seems to contradict it: 'I'm not the aggressor, she is.' (This perhaps ties in with the fact that he prefers it when the woman gets on top and does everything for him.)

What about his wife's desire, his wife being the other candidate for the Other with a capital *O*? About this we know nothing from the case study. Could it be that she would rather he seek sexual satisfaction with someone else? The remark he makes about the passionate-looking woman he saw in a restaurant the day before, who he thought would immediately respond if he made an overture, might incline us to think that he is a man who has affairs. Perhaps this is just fine with his wife? Indeed, perhaps his wife—in a somewhat typical hysterical fashion—can only continue to desire her husband when she sees that he desires other women? If the dream can be understood as staging the wife's wishes, then it would seem that her wish is for him to be desired by other women. But whether she wants anyone to have sexual satisfaction is less clear. This is all somewhat pointless speculation, however, as Sharpe tells us nothing about the wife....

If we leave aside the idea that the unconscious desire in the dream is the Other's desire, since we don't know what the Other's desire is here, we could speculate that the patient's unconscious desire here is to be desired without having to provide jouissance to anyone else. Which strongly resembles an hysterical position: "No jouissance for the Other!"

Yet the hysteric's position is a bit different in that, although wanting to be the cause of the partner's desire, but not the cause of the partner's jouissance, she is constantly on the lookout for a desire in her partner for someone else, or even inciting such a desire. Why? To ensure that his desire is still alive, that he is not dead, as partners so often are. Ella Sharpe's patient does not seem to be looking for that, at least not in this specific dream.[10]

Are the Other and the Phallus Identical Here?

Sharpe's patient identifies his wife with the phallus, according to Lacan. His wife, who he keeps on the sidelines, above the fray, is preserved from the dream's action. In the dream, we might say that she represents the phallus as a jouissance that may potentially be refound, that might be

---

[10] The hysteric is almost sure to be disappointed by an obsessive, who cannot commit to making her the central cause of his desire, always needing to slip from one object to another, and generally trying to hide this fact from her. If she manages to prove to herself that his desire is still alive, because she can detect or incite a desire in him for someone else, this nevertheless torments her, as she is not in the position she would like to be in relation to his desire and has to make do with jealousy—which is still, of course, a form of jouissance, but not as good as what she's looking for.

For an obsessive to show her that she is the central cause of his desire would, to his mind, be to kowtow to what he believes her desire to be—that is, kowtow to her desire and please her—something he avoids at all costs. Thus the position of Sharpe's patient might, alternatively, reflect the obsessive's *cri de guerre*: "I wouldn't give her the satisfaction of knowing I desire her. The Other will not get off on me! She'll get nothing from me!" (Lacan, in saying that he can't allow his wife or analyst to be castrated, seems to be situating him as a pervert, for whom the Other has to be complete.)

recovered. In that sense, we can try to understand what Lacan means what he says that what the neurotic refuses to accept more than anything else is that the Other be castrated, in other words, that the Other be deprived of jouissance. The "mainspring of neurosis is not to want the Other to be castrated" (S6, p. 229).

The patient's wife, who stands in here for the mother as a sort of absolute Other—for she is put on a pedestal and kept unsullied, unravished—must be preserved at all costs, for she represents jouissance that cannot be lost, alienated, or castrated (S6, p. 226). She is the queen he refused to put at risk or sacrifice—recall that Lacan embraces Sharpe's characterization of this analysis (and perhaps other analyses) as a sort of game of chess, and refers to the endgame in chess where there are very few pieces left on the board. He says:

> As I was reading this passage, it led me to think, "That's very nice. One should compare the whole unfolding of an analysis to a game of chess." Why? Because what is most beautiful and salient in the game of chess is that each of the pieces is a signifying element. The game involves a series of moves that respond to each other, based on the nature of these signifiers, each having its own characteristic movement based on its position as a signifier; and what occurs is the progressive reduction of the number of signifiers left in the game. One could, after all, describe an analysis in the same way, by saying that what we need to do is eliminate a sufficient number of signifiers for there to remain few enough of them for us to clearly sense where among them the subject's position within the structure lies. Having returned to this notion later, I believe that it can, in effect, take us quite far. (S6, p. 203)

Certain players feel they cannot win if they sacrifice their queen to take out one of their opponent's pieces, yet that is precisely what often allows one to win. We might be reminded here again of the Biblical notion that if you try to save your life, you will lose it (Matthew 16:25). If we slip from "life" to "wife" here—and this is, in my experience, a common slip of the tongue made by married men who speak English—we see that *to attempt to save one's queen is to lose the game, that is, to lose everything.*

How do we explain the function of the castration complex? We have to know in what way the assumption by the subject of a position in the signifying order implies the loss or sacrifice of one of his signifiers. (S6, p. 196)

The signifier he refuses to lose here is the queen, which Lacan associates with the phallus, and with the patient's wife and analyst in this case. He refers here to the "female partner qua Other with a capital *O*" (S6, pp. 204–5). And on page 225 he refers to the phallus as "the signifier that takes on all values."[11]

Why can't the obsessive allow the Other to be castrated, cut down to size, taken down a notch? If he did, he would have to grapple with the lack in the Other!

The child initially believes the Other knows all its thoughts. The psychotic continues to suspect or even be convinced of that, but the neurotic comes to realize—through an encounter with the Other's lack of knowledge—that he can hide things from the Other with greater or lesser ease. "Keeping the Other in the dark ... is absolutely foundational in one's relation to the Other. [...] Hence the importance of the moment at which he realizes that the Other may not know. This 'not knowing' in the Other is correlated with the very constitution of the subject's unconscious" (S6, p. 240).[12]

The discovery of lack in the Other—lack of knowledge, and lack at the root of the Other's desire for something other than the child—is

---

[11] This is not, I think, the same phenomenon as the notion in popular culture expressed by the term "trophy wife." In the popular culture notion, a man selects a woman whom he believes other people will envy and think of as a fabulous catch. They will think of him as lucky for having managed to seduce her or otherwise reel her in. She may also embody all of his losses for him, and the hope of, through her, getting back what he lost, but she may be primarily reduced to a symbol in his mind, a symbol of what others desire, and that will thus make him look good to other people.

[12] This implies, once again, that there is no unconscious in psychosis. (The refusal to imagine the Other as castrated would seem to be an imaginary project not a symbolic one.) "The Other's desire, specifically the mother's desire, is not symbolized" in psychosis (S5, p. 455). What this leads to, in the case of a psychotic subject, is that "the Other's speech does not pass into his unconscious; instead the Other, as the locus of speech, talks to him constantly.... The 'it is speaking' [*ça parle*] that is in the neurotic subject's unconscious is outside for the psychotic subject" (p. 455). Lacan talks about the delusion of jealousy as an attempt to attribute a desire to the Other, "to instate in the Other the desire I don't have, because I am psychotic, because nowhere was the essential metaphor produced that gives the Other's desire its primordial signifier, the phallus" (p. 456). The psychotic does not have access to all "four cardinal points of the definition of desire" (L Schema, or child, mother, Father, phallus; p. 458), hence does not have access to desire, strictly speaking.

traumatizing. It is a major turning point in the coming into being of the subject. All neurotics, whether obsessive, hysterical, or phobic, strive very hard, at least at times, to avoid seeing or to cover over the lack in the Other! We shall see a striking example of this in Chap. 8.

Supervising Sharpe

Sharpe extrapolates in many ways, assuming that the patient must have seen this or that as a child—for example, his sister's and/or his mother's genitals from below—and Lacan often gives her the benefit of the doubt, insofar as he considers her to be a fine analyst, and privy to a great deal more information about the patient than we are. Yet he sometimes expresses his incredulity at conclusions she jumps to.

Let us observe that, even if Lacan does seem to be somewhat intrigued by the analogy between psychoanalysis and the game of chess, he does quip that this perhaps says more about Ella Sharpe herself than about analysis more generally: "it is her own intentions that are expressed in this term 'corner'" (S6, p. 204).[13] I would conclude that what he means is that it is Sharpe herself who would like to corner her patient, and indeed checkmate him, so that he will have to spill the beans, finally let some emotion appear, for she obviously identifies emotion with truth.

Sharpe stresses that her patient is very controlled and never says anything without forethought, as if he were trying to prevent any feeling from ever appearing in his sessions. And she appears to be extremely frustrated by this, seizing any and every opportunity to tell him how aggressive he really is, viewing, as he does (she thinks) his penis as a "biting and boring thing" (Sharpe 1937, p. 146). She writes,

> I think the analysis might be compared to a long-drawn-out game of chess and that it will continue to be so until I cease to be the unconscious avenging father who is bent on cornering him, checkmating him, after which there is no alternative to death. (Sharpe 1937, p. 127)

---

[13] Note that Lacan does not necessarily understand what the English expression "to corner someone" means; he seems to suggest it means hitting the ball from one corner to the other of a tennis court, instead of simply trapping someone in a certain corner of the court.

Sharpe clearly concluded that, as a child, the patient wished his father dead, and his father then died, leaving the child with the impression that his wishes and aggression were omnipotent. She underscores

> his unconscious wish of the first years to get rid of his father, [and suggests that] only this wish alive again in the transference will ever moderate his omnipotent belief that he killed his father in reality. (Sharpe 1937, p. 127)

His aggressive wishes are so powerful that he must never express them, for if he did, they would totally destroy other people. Hence his inability to seal the deal on the tennis court, showing his superior ability by actually winning two sets in a row; and hence his inability to argue in court as a lawyer, for that would involve beating someone else—namely, the lawyer(s) for the opposition. To even wish to do so is to kill. Hence, all such wishes must be set aside, suppressed. To Sharpe's mind, the patient is full of aggression, but has repressed his aggressive impulses. She pounces on the slightest hint of aggression in his speech or dreams.

Lacan clearly finds this unjustified. He says:

> It seems to me that we cannot react to a case study that was written up and that we read in the same way as we talk to our students about their cases. If I were dealing with a student, I would speak much more severely in such an instance. I would say, "What could have possibly inspired you to say such a thing?" I would inquire as to where the countertransference came in. (S6, p. 202)

He criticizes Sharpe for taking things up so often at the imaginary level: at that of dyadic, rivalrous, competitive, aggressive relations (see S6, pp. 154, 188, and 193). Had she taken things up at the symbolic level, she might have focused more on the last words purportedly uttered by the patient's father: "Robert must take my place" (Robert being the name of the patient; p. 184).[14] What had he meant by them? Take the father's place in bed with the mother? Satisfy his mother in the father's stead? Or die like his father died? We know nothing about the father as a person, or

---

[14] The patient's name—assuming it is not a pseudonym—thus contains the verb "to rob," thus, to steal.

what kind of work he did, so we are left to speculate, or simply remain in the dark.

Lacan also feels it is unfortunate Sharpe did not take up the patient's obvious distortion of the following lines from *The Book of Common Prayer*: "We have left undone those things which we ought to have done; And we have done those things which we ought not to have done; And there is no health in us." Sharpe's patient says, instead: "Ah well, we have undone those things we ought to have done and there is no good thing in us" (Sharpe 1937, p. 136). In the patient's version, we see what Freud called "undoing": the attempt by the obsessive to undo what he did in an outburst of fury, in an unending pendulum swinging back and forth between love and hate (cf. the Rat Man's actions, SE X, p. 190).

Moreover, Lacan does not take the fact that the patient wet his bed after Sharpe commented on something, or that he grabbed his tennis partner by the throat after she interpretated something, as confirmation of the validity of her point of view (S6, 207–8). He takes them, rather, as acting out on his part.

6

The Lacanian Object

I mentioned in Chap. 2 that when Lacan uses the term "object" in this Seminar, he is almost always referring to another person, which was quite typical in most of psychoanalytic theory at the time (and perhaps even to this day). What he means by the object—and this is true for other concepts as well, like the phallus—keeps evolving over the course of his work, and we are left with a many-layered concept, instead of something with one clear meaning. Lacan's innovation in terminology in the 1950s was to reserve "object" for the little other or semblable. He was, of course, aware of the term "partial object" or "part-object" (see, for example, S6, p. 439, where it is contrasted with "total object"; see, also, *Écrits*, p. 505) introduced by Karl Abraham, which he embraces to some degree but also critiques for a variety of reasons, the simplest of which is found in *Écrits*:

> The notion of part-object seems to me to be the most accurate discovery analysis has made here, but it made it at the cost of postulating an ideal totalization of this object, thereby losing the benefit of the discovery. (p. 566)

Lacan clearly does not believe that human beings relate to other people as whole or total objects, we always being interested in or turned on by

B. Fink, *Lacan on Desire*, The Palgrave Lacan Series,
https://doi.org/10.1007/978-3-031-76386-1_6

some part of them, by something we see in them which is not the whole of them. Had he been a native speaker of English, he might have said we relate to others as "hole-objects."

Note that Lacan introduces a new term on pages 213–219 of Seminar VI: the "desired object." In the context in question, it is the mother's breast. He says that the mother's breast becomes a desired object, strictly speaking, insofar as the child feels it is deprived of it by its little brother or sister—that is, in competition with a semblable (i.e., little other). Lacan says here that the breast takes on "the special value of being desired at the same time as it makes the subject conscious of himself as deprived" (S6, p. 219). This is perhaps his very first step toward object a—that is, toward the object not as another person but as cause of desire. This desired object comes into being at the very moment the subject comes into being as lacking, as sensing that he is missing something. In other words, object a arises simultaneously with the split subject, $\cancel{S}$, with the divided or castrated subject. Later in the Seminar, he talks about the object, not "of desire" but "the object in desire" (p. 327), adding further on that "What I am calling the place of the object in desire is completely new territory" (S6, p. 346).

Here, the formula that I proposed earlier—

$$\frac{a}{-\varphi}$$

—is especially relevant. The object comes to the fore as the subject begins to experience himself as castrated. And just as minus phi can be situated in the sliver of Venn diagrams for the subject (see Fig. 6.1), indicating what the subject feels he or she is missing, it can also be situated in the sliver of the diagram for the Other (see Fig. 6.2; S6, pp. 214–5), and in the intersection between the two, where Lacan also situates object a (see Fig. 6.3; cf. S11, p. 211). Object a arises in the place of the lack in both the subject and the Other.

The subject is lacking in being because he situates his being in the desired object! To jump ahead eight years: Lacan proposes that we understand object a as the subject's *Dasein* (S14, p. 396)! Object a is the last refuge of his jouissance, of his being as jouissance or jouissance being.

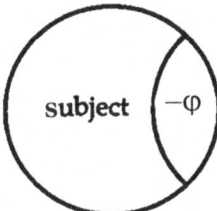

Fig. 6.1 The subject and –φ

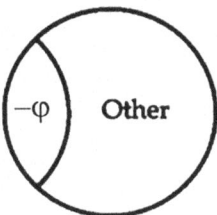

Fig. 6.2 The Other and –φ

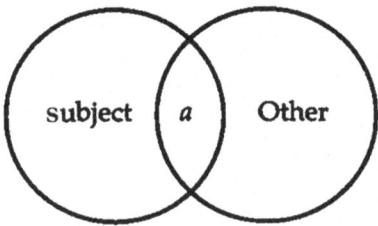

Fig. 6.3 Object *a* as the intersection of the subject and the Other

Recall that later in his work, Lacan comes up with yet another definition of object *a*: *plus-de-jouir*, surplus jouissance. (It first appears in Seminar XVI.)

If you have often found yourselves confused by object *a*, welcome to the club! Lacan often proposes concepts and mathemes, which he works and reworks over the course of almost 30 years, layering one meaning upon another, without ever explicitly rejecting older meanings. This is true of his formulas for fantasy and the drive, for the phallus, and one might even say for the subject.

One thing to note, at least here, is that when a matheme is included in his written texts in italics, this implies that it is imaginary, and we see the "a" of object *a* written in italics for a very long time in Lacan's work (the barred subject is, too, and Lacan even comments on that fact on page 479 of Seminar VI). It is only perhaps toward the very end that "a" of object **a** is written in Roman type, and sometimes in bold—although we don't know if it was Lacan or his editor who introduced that typographical convention.[1]

Consider the following list of objects *a* found in *Écrits* (p. 693) and the equation he makes between the object and the subject's being:

> the mamilla, the feces, the phallus (as an imaginary object), and the urinary flow. (An unthinkable list, unless we add, as I do, the phoneme, the gaze, the voice ... and the nothing.) For isn't it plain to see that the characteristic of being partial, rightly emphasized in objects, is applicable not because these objects are part of a total object, which the body is assumed to be, but because they only partially represent the function that produces them?
>
> A common characteristic of these objects as I formulate them is that they have no specular image, in other words, no alterity. This is what allows them to be the "stuff" or, better put, the lining [...] of the very subject people take to be the subject of consciousness. For this subject, who thinks he can accede to himself by designating himself in the statement, is nothing but such an object. Ask someone with writer's block about the anxiety he experiences and he will tell you who the turd *is* in his fantasy.[2]

The turd in his fantasy is him: his subjectivity is located in the object. The object takes the place of his being, occupies the place of his *Dasein*. He is nothing without the object, nothing but lack, nothing but an empty placeholder, nothing but the empty set.

---

[1] Note, too, that *d*, for desire, on the graph is in italics, suggesting that at this stage Lacan views desire as imaginary, at least in some important sense. One of the confusing things is that he later discusses the letter d, as standing for delusion, and this d is not in italics! I was not present at the Seminar when he wrote the letter on the blackboard, so I cannot say whether he truly did or didn't write it in italics. This is just one of the many difficulties in interpreting the mathemes and concepts.

[2] The quote continues: "It is to this object that cannot be grasped in the mirror that the specular image lends its clothes. A substance caught in the net of shadow, and which, robbed of its shadow-swelling volume, holds out once again the tired lure of the shadow as if it were substance" (*Écrits*, p. 693).

Much the same notion is found elsewhere in *Écrits*:

> These objects, whether part-objects or not, but certainly signifying objects—the breast, excrement, and the phallus—are no doubt won or lost by the subject; he is destroyed by them or preserves them, but above all he *is* these objects, according to the place where they function in his fundamental fantasy. (p. 513)

Complicating matters further, consider the "three types of little *a*" provided in Seminar VI on pp. 382–8: the pregenital object (nipple and turd), the phallus (imaginary), and delusion (d).

This list turns out to be not that different from lists of objects we find elsewhere, given the pregenital objects he mentions; but by including the category of delusion, Lacan perhaps first introduces here the idea of the voice as one of the objects *a*. Under the heading of the phallus, Lacan discusses mutilation, the most common form of which is circumcision, but all forms of which inscribe the subject in the social order: "Initiation rites [...] change the meaning of the subject's natural desires" (S6, p. 385). All three "types of little *a*" involve cutting: cutting off of the child's access to the breast; cutting turds; cutting into the body; and cutting off of speech, interrupted sentences, and suspended signification.[3] Indeed, "these objects are very precisely selected insofar as they manifest in their form [the very] structure of cutting" (p. 383).[4]

Adding yet one more layer to the concept of object *a*, Lacan says: "little *a* is the Other's desire" (or what the Other desires) (S6 p. 420); the object of desire is the Other's desire (p. 478). We try to fill the lack in ourselves with the Other's desire for us.

A whole book could be written on the development and evolution of the concept of object *a* in Lacan's thought. I even thought seriously about doing so after writing *The Lacanian Subject*, but decided to turn to more directly clinical matters instead. I may get around to it someday, since I have a fairly complete table of contents for it!

---

[3] His fascination with cutting only grows as time goes on, and perhaps explains in part his interest in filmmaking, which obviously involves cutting in a big way: cutting scenes!

[4] "Being is the same thing as cutting. Cutting renders being present in the symbolic" (S6, p. 408).

Part III

Lacan's Reading of *Hamlet*

7

Introductory Considerations

Disclaimers

Interpreting Shakespeare's play, *Hamlet*, is a minefield. As Lacan himself admits, so many wildly different explanations of the play have been proffered that it is hard to believe so many contradictory things could be said about one and the same play. Dan Collins has gone so far as to characterize *Hamlet* as the play of interpretation itself, as a play designed to require the audience to engage in the act of interpretation.[1] One thing we can safely say from the outset is that there are interpretations with virtually no textual justification, and others that can, at least, point to specific passages in the play that support them. This is true of people's interpretations of Lacan's work too! Some are simply wild, some are more disciplined.

I personally find that Lacan's grasp of Shakespearean English (not to mention more contemporary English) is at times shaky and even faulty. Yet the play was written with so many double, triple, and quadruple

---

[1] *Hamlet* is, Collins (2022) writes, "an *object* of interpretation. The audience must interpret. I believe that *Hamlet* is the first work in literature that calls upon the reader to interpret in the modern sense of the word."

B. Fink, *Lacan on Desire*, The Palgrave Lacan Series,
https://doi.org/10.1007/978-3-031-76386-1_7

entendres that even native English speakers very familiar with Shakespeare's usage are hard-pressed to explicate it. There are, moreover, rather different versions available (the quarto edition from 1603 and the First Folio edition, published in 1623, based on a second 1604 quarto edition), which makes interpretation a dodgy business. You cite a passage in the text, and then it turns out to be different or not even exist in another edition. A paper I wrote on Hamlet in the 1990s relied heavily on one edition and makes no sense when compared with the other edition.[2]

This is true of Lacan's Seminars, too. If you read through my notes to Seminar VI, included in the appendix to the present volume, you will see how this complicates the translation and interpretation of Lacan's work.

Headline Claims

Lacan devotes seven classes of this Seminar to a detailed discussion of the play. As we often find in Lacan's Seminars, the discussion begins in a very focused way, and then meanders in various different directions, which rarely seem to lead to definitive conclusions. He had apparently planned to spend about four classes on the play, and after seven he seems to drop *Hamlet* only to return to it at the end of a class a month later. Much the same thing can be said about his reading of Plato's *Symposium* in Seminar VIII: many brilliant things get said along the way, but it takes a great deal of work on the reader's part to extract a specific interpretation of the text from his myriad divagations and he keeps returning to it here and there later in the Seminar.[3]

Lacan takes a great many stabs at what is behind the arras (i.e., curtain) in *Hamlet*, but does not seem to make any definitive statement as to the meaning of the play by the end of the seven classes. Or, rather, he makes many large claims, but often leaves them by the wayside as he proceeds:

---

[2] It can be found in Fink (2014a, pp. 86–99).
[3] For a detailed exploration of his discussion of the *Symposium*, see Fink (2016).

- Whereas the dream about the dead father was the "confrontation with death" (S6, p. 94), "the tragedy of *Hamlet* is the encounter with death" (p. 292).
- It is "the tragedy [or: drama] of desire" (S6, pp. 249 and 306).
- "The tragedy is founded on the subject's relationship to truth" (S6, p. 401).
- It is the encounter with the signifier of the lack in the Other—that is, with the fundamental uncertainty of all knowledge and truth, the fundamental unreliability of the Other, of people, of discourse itself, leading to Hamlet's conclusion (in my own words) that "All is lies, and everyone is an 'arrant knave,' myself included."
- Since truth is called into question, there being no Truth with a capital *T*, Hamlet must encounter something that resides beyond the locus of truth (which is flawed, lacking, unreliable): "the moment of truth" (S6, p. 294), "the moment of the encounter with himself, with his *will*" (p. 295; my emphasis). "What is involved is, in the final analysis, not the level of truth but the moment of truth" (p. 314), which is a sort of rendezvous or appointment with fate.
- Desire is inextricably bound up with mourning (mourning the loss of the phallus; S6, p. 345).
- *Hamlet* is as great a tale as Sophocles' *Oedipus Rex*.
- It is the play that, *par excellence*, juxtaposes knowledge and desire.
- It shows us the "slow birthing of the necessary castration" that Hamlet had not undergone prior to the play.
- "Hamlet [the character] is purely and simply the place of desire" (S6, p. 289).
- "*Hamlet* [the play] brings out the different levels, indeed the very framework [...] in which desire is situated. The place of desire is so excellently and exceptionally articulated in *Hamlet* that everybody [...] recognizes himself in it.[4] The structure of the play is a type of network or bird catcher's net in which man's desire is caught. And his desire is essentially articulated there in the coordinates that Freud reveals to us—namely, in connection with the Oedipus complex and castration" (S6, p. 257).

---

[4] I can't say I've ever recognized myself in it …

- *Hamlet* shows us how man must find his desire, at great personal cost and suffering (S6, p. 257).
- Hamlet finds his desire in competition with Laertes. It is the struggle with the imaginary other, his rival, that finally allows him to assume castration, assume his position as a subject: "This is I, Hamlet the Dane" (*Hamlet*, V, i, 244–5).
- "*Hamlet* is an illusion" (S6, p. 272) and its hero "is a mode of discourse" (p. 273).
- Hamlet "is a character who is made up of something: the empty place in which we can situate our ignorance. This is what is important, because a situated ignorance is not purely negative—it renders the unconscious present, no more, no less" (S6, p. 275).
- Hamlet, like most obsessives, is always living on the Other's time, the Other's watch, not on his own. Yet he has both obsessive and hysterical features!
- "What Hamlet is constantly dealing or grappling with is a desire which is far from being his own. As it is situated in the play, it is the desire, not *for* his mother, but *of* his mother—that is, it is his mother's desire" (S6, p. 280). "His mother's desire here takes on anew for him the value of something that can in no way be dominated, moved, or eliminated" (p. 282).
- Ophelia is the phallus, both etymologically and in the play (S6, p. 304).
- It is Hamlet's father who pours poison into Hamlet's ears! He is responsible, in the end, for poisoning his own son, for the death of his own son. (Lacan then pours poison into our ears, too, when he complains about a Marxist idiot…. Lacan thereby poisons his own students, murdering their innocence.

Such are Lacan's big headline claims about the play, a number of which I will explicate in what follows.

Hamlet and the Graph of Desire

We learn a number of things about the Graph of Desire in the course of the discussion of *Hamlet*, including that it is the lower half of the Graph that concerns what is "accessible to consciousness" (S6, p. 392), and that it is in the upper half that the unconscious is created and located (p. 309), the unconscious as something that is "inaccessible to consciousness" (p. 392). The lower half concerns demand, and the upper half desire (pp. 282–3). The lower half concerns alienation, and the upper half separation ("the dialectic of separation"; p. 449).

And we find the "circuit," as he calls it, of what goes on in the unconscious (S6, p. 285) in the trajectory between desire, fantasy, the signifier of the lack in the Other, and the drive. The unconscious circuit

> begins on the right, at the extremity of the unconscious vector, provisionally denoted Δ. It rises to the level of the message, $S(\bar{A})$, continues over to the code ($\cancel{S} \Diamond D$), drops back down to the level of desire, d, and from there heads toward fantasy ($\cancel{S} \Diamond a$). This is the circuit of the formation of desire at the level of the unconscious, and these are the stages it goes through and the directions in which it goes through them. (pp. 285–6)

I don't believe Lacan ever shows us how Hamlet goes through these stages in precisely this order, however.

Lacan asserts that in most cases a subject can breathe easy and desire between the Graph's two main horizontal lines (S6, p. 300). But Hamlet unfortunately encountered "something from the real Other": his mother "who is less desire than gluttony and even engulfment" (p. 300; she presumably did not manifest a proper lack). This was a "revelation" to him: he discovered that she was a "man-eater" (p. 301)! This presumably brought him down to the lower level of the Graph, crushing his desire. We'll turn to that further on.

Comparing and Contrasting *Hamlet* with *Oedipus*

Lacan begins his discussion of the play by comparing and contrasting *Hamlet* with *Oedipus Rex*, perhaps because Freud brings both of them up in the same chapter of *The Interpretation of Dreams*, a chapter serendipitously entitled "Dreams of the death of persons of whom the dreamer is fond" (S6, p. 235). This dovetails quite nicely with Lacan's preoccupation with dreams regarding death thus far in the Seminar.

He highlights the fact that, in the Oedipus myth, something of very great importance is *not* known (Oedipus does not know that he has killed his father and slept with his mother), whereas in *Hamlet* something very important *is* known (that Hamlet senior was killed by his brother Claudius, who is now married to and sleeping with Gertrude, his former sister-in-law).

$$\frac{\text{He did not know}}{\text{Oedipus (the son)}} \qquad \frac{\text{He did know}}{\text{Hamlet senior}}$$

Lacan immediately takes it for granted that the ghost is not a demon or devil of some kind that has come to mislead Hamlet, and that Hamlet should take what the ghost says as gospel truth. Not everyone seems to agree with Lacan on that score (see Collins 2022). The play is set in pre-Reformation times, perhaps between 1016–1042 when England owed tribute to Denmark (having been conquered by Swein's son Cnut who took the crown). The idea of Purgatory as a physical place became a formal part of Roman Catholic teaching in the late 11th century, and is alluded to here by the ghost, when he says:

> I am thy father's spirit,
> Doomed for a certain term to walk the night
> And for the day confined to fast in fires
> Till the foul crimes done in my days of nature
> Are burnt and purged away. (I, v, 14–18)

Shakespeare's post-Reformation audience might well have viewed the ghost's appearance and the tale he tells of his woes as typical Catholic silliness, certainly as non-Anglican. They might not have considered the ghost as a source of sure information as Lacan does. Hamlet says it is either "a spirit of health or goblin damned" (I, iv, 44), and Horatio worries that it may drive him mad and tempt him to jump off a cliff into the sea (I, iv, 77–86). Nevertheless, by the next scene Hamlet asserts to Horatio that "It is an honest ghost—that let me tell you" (I, v, 154). But he later says, "The spirit that I have seen / May be a devil" (II, ii, 627–9). Later still, "a damned ghost" (III, ii, 87).

Be that as it may, the point is that Lacan contrasts the plays as regards knowledge, asserting that Oedipus did not know, whereas Hamlet did. He does not indicate at that point in the Seminar (S6, pp. 242–3) that knowledge is not situated in the same generation in the two plays: in the Oedipus story, it is the son who does not know, and in *Hamlet*, it is the late King Hamlet who knows, and then communicates this knowledge to his son. (Note, however, that both father and son are named Hamlet.)

Lacan also contrasts the situation in *Hamlet* with the dream about the dead father: "The first thread in *Hamlet* is that the father quite clearly knows that he is dead *as his brother Claudius wished*, Claudius having wanted to take his place" (S6, p. 241; emphasis added).

The difference in generations is pointed out a hundred pages later, but not as regards the location of knowledge. Lacan says,

> In *Oedipus*, the crime occurs during the hero's generation. In *Hamlet*, it occurs in the prior generation. In *Oedipus*, the crime is committed when the hero does not know what he is doing and is in some sense guided by *fatum* [fate]. In *Hamlet*, the crime is committed in a deliberate manner, since it is committed through treachery. (S6, p. 342)

In any case, Lacan stresses that the implicit question in both stories, "Who killed the father?", is answered in *Hamlet* right from the get-go, whereas in *Oedipus* it takes a great deal of time and effort for the question to be answered (S6, p. 297). This is a bit of a stretch, because no one seems to be asking who killed Hamlet's father at the beginning of *Hamlet*, the official story—which no one seems to impugn—being that he died one day out in his orchard, having been bitten by a poisonous snake:

> 'Tis given out that, sleeping in my orchard,
> A serpent stung me; (I, v, 42–3)[5]

Hamlet, while talking with the ghost, *does* exclaim upon hearing the news that Claudius murdered Hamlet's father, "O my prophetic soul! My uncle!" (I, v, 48). So we can assume that at least Hamlet had *suspected* foul play, even if he had never mentioned this to anyone.

Let us note that, despite Hamlet's exceedingly high praise of his father, his father is hardly squeaky clean. He must have committed some crimes, about which we know nothing, for he mentions "the foul crimes done in my days of nature" (I, v, 17), which might incline us to think he is referring to his youth or at least earlier days; yet he also says that he was struck down "in the blossoms of [his] sin" (I, v, 76) and "with all [his] imperfections" (I, v, 79), which makes it sound like he was still blithely sinning away when he was murdered. Lacan seems to conclude that, whatever his crimes, they were not sins against his wife, to whom he was completely faithful, but crimes of some other sort. Hamlet himself tells us that Claudius cut his father down with all his crimes still to his discredit:

> [Claudius] took my father grossly, full of bread;
> With all his crimes broad blown, as flush as May. (III, iii, 86)

According to the Catholic tradition, he would have needed to confess to and receive absolution for those crimes if he wished to go to heaven, but he was killed before he could do so. Hamlet senior says:

> Cut off, even in the blossoms of my sin,
> Unhouseled, disappointed, unaneled,
> No reck'ning made, but sent to my account
> With all my imperfections on my head.

---

[5] Note that, if we take the orchard to represent the Garden of Eden, the serpent is the Devil (or Satan) in the tree of the knowledge of good and evil, which perhaps explains why the father knows.

It is only later that Lacan quips that "Like all men, this king may, of course, have been a serious rascal" (S6, p. 297), and only much later that he raises questions about the father's potential responsibility for the crimes committed by Claudius and Gertrude (p. 403).[6]

Whatever the case may be—whether Hamlet senior was a serious rascal or an eminent statesman—Lacan says that he "is someone who has not paid for the crime of existing" (S6, p. 247), which we might interpret here as original sin, or as something more existential, Lacan having also said that "Hamlet [...] knows that he is guilty for being. [...] Hamlet knows what it means to have committed the crime of existing" (pp. 245–6). Lacan goes on to say that "Hamlet can neither pay in his father's stead nor leave the debt unpaid" (p. 247). What's a boy to do? He's between a rock and a hard place.

---

[6] Collins (2022) goes so far as to claim that no one in the play, except for Hamlet, has anything nice to say about the late King Hamlet, and that he was "a reckless king, who drank, napped away his afternoons, and wagered half his kingdom on single combat with the king of Norway," the elder Fortinbras. Yet Horatio—the only person who remains faithful to Hamlet from the beginning to the end of the play—calls King Hamlet "valiant" (I, i, 96) and "a goodly king" (I, ii, 193), and informs us that the single combat with the elder Fortinbras resulted from a challenge made by Fortinbras, *not* by King Hamlet (coincidentally enough, Hamlet junior was born the day Hamlet senior defeated Fortinbras). Moreover, reveling and drinking is attributed *not* to King Hamlet, but to Claudius (I, iv, 9–11).

8

The Signifier of the Lack in the Other

Returning to the list of headline claims I provided in Chap. 7, let me take up the fourth item. Hamlet encounters the signifier of the lack in the Other here, according to Lacan, when the ghost tells him about the way in which he was murdered. Hamlet had presumably been thinking that all was well in the best of all possible worlds, everything was hunky-dory between his parents, but he was completely wrong. While his father was ostensibly in love with his mother—"With his wife [...] he went so far as to shield her face from 'the winds of heaven'" (I, ii, 141)—she betrayed him with his brother (no one says she cheated on her husband during his lifetime, but she switches husbands awfully fast). And his brother, who presumably respected him, was in fact plotting against him behind his back in the hope of taking both his crown and his queen.

This leads Hamlet to the following conclusion: "There's never a villain dwelling in all Denmark / But he's an arrant knave" (I, v, 23–4). ("Arrant" means thorough, notorious, unmitigated, or downright. The claim may sound tautological to our ears, but in Shakespeare's time, "villain" was close in meaning to villager: unpolished or rustic village dweller.) Hamlet even tells Ophelia that *he himself* is an arrant knave later; and he quips elsewhere, "Use every man after his desert [i.e., according to what he

© The Author(s), under exclusive license to Springer Nature Switzerland AG 2025
B. Fink, *Lacan on Desire*, The Palgrave Lacan Series,
https://doi.org/10.1007/978-3-031-76386-1_8

deserves, according to his merit] and who shall 'scape whipping?" (II, ii, 555–7).

According to Lacan, Hamlet thus encountered "the absolute duplicity of what had seemed to [him] to be the very epitome and essence of beauty and truth" (S6, p. 297). In short, his whole world was rocked. "It is the irremediable, absolute, unfathomable betrayal of love—of the purest love, the love this king had" (p. 297–8).

The ground was somehow cut out from under Hamlet (which, centuries later, would be a good reason to go into analysis!). He was forced to realize that his mother was lascivious, not a pure, virginal Madonna. Indeed, the status of women in general was overturned for him. A wife, nay, a queen, was suddenly no better than a whore in his eyes.

This is why Lacan emphasizes Hamlet's encounter with Ophelia shortly after hearing the revelations made by his father's ghost. According to Lacan, Hamlet can no longer recognize Ophelia, after having been in love with her for some time (S6, p. 317). He is in a sorry, disheveled sartorial state, seems totally disoriented, and unable to fathom who and what she is, despite staring at her for quite some time.

According to Lacan, something is shaken up here at the level of his own self-image, as connected to the other's image, *i(a)*. Lacan refers to what Hamlet experiences here as something like "depersonalization," as if he began to ask himself: If women are trash, then what am I? (S6, p. 320). Am I, too, nothing but trash? He later tells Ophelia that he, like everyone else, is an arrant knave:

> I am myself indifferent honest,
> but yet I could accuse me of such things
> that it were better my mother had not borne me:
> I am very proud, revengeful, ambitious, with more offenses
> at my beck than I have thoughts to put them in,
> imagination to give them shape,
> or time to act them in.
> What should such fellows as I do
> crawling between earth and heaven?
> We are arrant knaves all;
> believe none of us. (III, i, 132–40)

Lacan takes the scene with Ophelia at face value, whereas one could easily argue that it is an act on Hamlet's part designed, perhaps (as Collins 2022 suggests), to test Ophelia's reliability and fidelity to him, or simply to dupe everyone. He was completely fine just moments before, in full possession of his faculties, and warned Horatio that he was about to put on a serious act, asking Horatio to swear not to rat him out:

> How strange or odd some'er I bear myself
> (As I perchance hereafter shall think meet
> To put an antic disposition on). (I, v, 190–2)

Taking this scene at face value, and not as a show put on by Hamlet to fool everyone as to his feelings and intentions, Lacan calls this the "first stage" of the object-relation: "estrangement" (S6, p. 317).

This is why Lacan considers the female characters in Shakespeare's plays before and after *Hamlet* to see how Shakespeare's conception of women evolved up to this point—that including Ophelia and Gertrude—and after this point. He suggests that both before and after *Hamlet* we tend to see women who are more boy-girl or girl-boy (S6, p. 303). He doesn't, for some unknown reason, mention in this context Kate in *The Taming of the Shrew*.

One of the few biographical details about Shakespeare that Lacan mentions is the one cited by Freud: Shakespeare apparently wrote *Hamlet* right after the death of his own father (S6, pp. 238–9). If this biographical detail is true, Shakespeare had just lost the "shield" mentioned earlier, the barrier between himself and death, the barrier "with respect to the absolute master, death." "A father is required to stabilize the subject's desire," Lacan tells us later in the Seminar (p. 414). He does not dwell on any of the other (admittedly precious few) details we know about Shakespeare's life, but we might wonder whether Shakespeare's mother immediately began to have relations with another man after her husband's death and whether Shakespeare himself thus felt his own world rocked, as his hero does.

No Other of the Other, No Truth with a Capital *T*, No Guarantee

The foundations of Hamlet's world are shaken up as he inadvertently stumbles upon the fact "that there is no Other of the Other" (S6, p. 298), which Lacan terms "The big secret of psychoanalysis." As Lacan puts it:

> The problem is that I have absolutely no guarantee that this Other, owing to what he has in his system, can give me back, if I may express myself thus, what I gave him—namely, his being and his essence as truth. As I told you, there is no Other of the Other. There is no signifier in the Other that can, in this case, answer for [*répondre de*] what I am. (S6, p. 299)

Prior to the encounter with the ghost, Hamlet purportedly thought there was such a thing as Truth with a capital *T*, a guarantee of knowledge. He granted the position of guarantor to his parents or to the throne, but something was not given back to him. Rather than telling him who he was—the Prince of Denmark, next in line for the sacred throne—they shut him out.

For "there is no other guarantee of truth than the Other's good faith … The subject continues to depend on utter and complete faith in the Other" (S6, p. 395), "on the Other's goodwill" (p. 377). This is what Hamlet realizes he can no longer do, having come to realize that everyone is lying to him (except Horatio and maybe Ophelia, but she is being puppeteered, as it were, by Polonius). He can no longer have "faith in [their] speech" or "count on the Other" (p. 372).

According to Lacan, Hamlet's encounter with the signifier of the lack in the Other keeps him questioning the Other throughout the play, his mother being the most significant instantiation of the Other here. His implicit question would be, "Who am I to her? What does she want of me?" Let us plot this on the Graph (see Fig. 1.1).

The move beyond the Other illustrated by the *Che vuoi?* arrows amounts, according to Lacan, to the real or ultimate question a child asks its parents. The child's multiple and repeated questions, "What do you want?" and "What do you want from me?" boil down to "What is my place in all of this?" Hamlet's "question," and Lacan views this question as being posed in Hamlet's long tirade to his mother in Act III, Scene IV, is "Where do I fit in?"

Lacan's discussion here seems to imply that there are essentially two kinds of answers the neurotic can receive to the question, "Who am I to my mother? What does she want from me?" In other words, the mOther can respond in two different ways. Graphically speaking, she can respond at a higher or a lower level, she can elevate or bring down her child. According to Lacan—and this is one of the points in his interpretation with which I do not agree, but which nevertheless illustrates the workings of his Graph of Desire—the response provided by Hamlet's mother to Hamlet's implicit question "Why don't you throw the toad out," is as follows: "I just can't, I'm a sex maniac—that's just the way I am, I need a man all the time." Lacan situates this response on the Graph at the level of $s(A)$, the signification that comes from the Other: the meaning given by the mOther, the explanation provided by the mother *about herself.*

Gertrude's response, as Lacan sees it, does not concern Hamlet—she does not, for example, say, "Why don't you mind your own business?" or "You are not enough for me, I cannot live without someone else in my life"—but rather simply describes Gertrude herself: "That's just the way I am."

Lacan goes very far in this direction, saying of Gertrude that "She is simply a gaping cunt. When one [man or penis] leaves, another enters" (S6, p. 287). I cannot see anything in the play that suggests she is so lascivious. And even if she were, what did she gain by changing husbands? Unless she was dissatisfied with King Hamlet, something that is never suggested in the play; indeed Hamlet says the opposite: "Why, she would hang on him / As if increase of appetite had grown / By what it fed on" (I, ii, 147–9).

She professes to Hamlet to be ashamed of having married her late husband's brother, but that is all:

Thou turn'st mine eyes into my very soul
And there I see such black…
As will not leave their tinct. (III, iv, 100–102)

Is this an admission of lasciviousness? Of faithlessness, perhaps, lack of allegiance and constancy.... Lacan may be suggesting that it is *Hamlet's* interpretation of his mother's behavior and speech that she has to have it all the time, for Lacan never points to any textual evidence for this claim.

Whether Lacan is right about Gertrude or not, he suggests that Hamlet was in need of an answer at some other level, or even no response at all. Lacan maintains that the neurotic must be confronted with the fact that there is no signifier in the Other that can "answer for (*répondre de*) his place as a subject" (S6, p. 377; "The Other replies: S($\cancel{A}$); p. 300)."*Répondre de*" should, I think, be understood quite forcefully here: "account for" or "take responsibility for." The signifier at issue is one that would not merely tell you what you are, but that would take you under its wing, define you, protect you, and constitute your *raison d'être*.

There is no such signifier. But not every mother helps her children realize this. Some mothers lead their children to believe that there *is* such a signifier and that it's *mom*. When, according to Lacan, Hamlet surreptitiously slips Gertrude the question, "What's my place in all this?" she doesn't say, "Damned if I know, and anyway you're old enough to figure it out for yourself." Hamlet's mother never answers his questions with a "How should I know?"[1] Instead she says, at least these are the very words Lacan puts in her mouth, "I am what I am; in my case there's nothing to be done, I'm a true genital personality—I know nothing of mourning" (S6, p. 286).

The point is that the mOther's discourse here has to do with herself, her own identity and her own characteristics. It concretizes something about the mOther—and it is plain to see that it concerns lack: according to Lacan, she says she has to be "getting it" all the time. But the answer is incommensurate with the question as Lacan understands it. If you ask your mother what you mean to her, and she answers by saying she loves petting cats and, every time your discourse is a fairly transparent cover for the same what-do-I-mean-to-you type question, she answers in the same general way, talking about herself, then she gives a particular kind of

---

[1] When "the Other no longer responds, the subject has to rely on (or: resort to) his own demand" (S5, p. 451).

meaning to your question, and the meaning of your speech is always determined retroactively in the same concrete way.

You may think your questions are about some sort of larger life-related issue, but the type of response you receive may prove them to be "about" something else. Your mOther here decides the meaning of the question you formulated, using the code made available to you by the Other as language; your enunciation comes into being as conveying a specific message on the basis of her response to it.

Thus, according to Lacan, Hamlet's mother converts Hamlet's discourse, Hamlet's repeatedly expressed desire to know where he fits in, into demand pure and simple—that is, into a demand for attention and love. All speech, ultimately, according to Lacan, makes a request or demand, and all demands are, regardless of their apparent content, demands for love. By converting Hamlet's desire into demand, Gertrude flattens it out, bringing it down to the lower level of the Graph of Desire.

Some other kind of response might have been able to bring Hamlet face to face with "the signifier of the lack in the Other," finally separating him from the symbolic order—that is, from the Other as language. This signifier of lack in the Other, $S(\cancel{A})$, is for all intents and purposes equivalent here to the signifier of (the Other's) desire, Φ, lack and desire being coextensive.

Hamlet looks to the Other for an answer about who and what he is. Instead of being given an answer at the level of meaning (as in the case in which Gertrude, according to Lacan, responds by talking about the kind of woman she is), he would, in the best of all possible worlds, be led to encounter the signifier of desire that just is—having no rhyme or reason, no explanation, justification, or *raison d'être*. The budding desire (*d*) that we see precariously perched on the "ladder" leading to the upper level of the Graph would become full-fledged due to its encounter with Φ as the signifier of desire—that is, as opaque signifier of the Other's desire. And a type of jouissance would become possible that is correlated with symbolic castration (see the upper horizontal arrow in Fig. 4.1).

Recall that desire arises only for those of us who perceive the Other as having a desire that is "obscure and opaque" (S6, p. 17), yet intriguing and important, not something to be taken at face value. What does this Other want of me, we wonder? We don't take for granted what the Other *says* he wants of us, but wonder what he *really* thinks of us and wants from us, which may be lightyears from what he says he thinks and wants.

Psychotics, on the other hand, take what their parents say they want at face value. It may be persecutory or not, but their parents' lack does not constitute a question to them, it is not a source of endless speculation and wondering for them. (Desire is thus immediately situated here by Lacan as something characteristic of neurosis, not psychosis.)

If I were to try to summarize what Lacan is hypothesizing about Hamlet, it is that, in his encounter with the ghost, Hamlet stumbles anew upon or runs up hard against *the lack in the Other*. In the rest of the play, we see him *trying to find its signifier*. He tries to locate it in his relationship with his mother (although she is the one that requests an audience with him), but she does not allow him to do so. He is only finally able to encounter the signifier of the lack in the Other owing to his struggle with Laertes in the graveyard scene.

Beyond the Lack in the Other to Its Signifier

How does that work? Here's *my* hypothesis: at this stage in his work, Lacan believes that the signifier of the lack in the Other is the symbolic phallus. The symbolic phallus is the signifier that is not included in the symbolic order, but that is always somehow in excess of it, outside of it. He more or less equates the two mathemes, $S(\cancel{A})$ and Φ, at this point in time, and perhaps more generally in his work.[2]

Lacan proposes that "Something real, which [the subject] has a hold on in an imaginary relationship, is raised to the pure and simple function of a signifier. This is the final and most profound meaning of castration as such" (S6, p. 367).[3] (The "something real" here would seem to be the penis.)

What we might say is that Hamlet is stuck at the level of the imaginary phallus, insofar as its place is held by the object, little *a*:

---

[2] Note that he also says that $S(\cancel{A})$ is shorthand for the castration complex.

[3] "The [imaginary] phallus is a privileged [or: exceptional or preferred] vital image raised up to the signification of a signifier" (S5, p. 471).

$$\frac{a}{(-\varphi)}$$

Who, then, are the little *a*s in the play? This is a complicated issue (just as it was in the dream recounted by Ella Sharpe's patient)!

Gertrude might be thought to be an object for Hamlet, even though we just saw her playing the role of the Other (or mOther). Hamlet's long discussion with her does not allow him, in Lacan's view, to go beyond, or perhaps better put, mourn the loss of his mother. We might object that he had long since lost her to his father. He might, like some children, have hoped, nevertheless, for some kind of rapprochement when his father died and he became king, but, instead, Gertrude remarried the father's brother and thus Hamlet's attachment to her became hopeless. And yet, still he did not lose hope—at least of making a better woman of her, of changing the fallen woman back into a Madonna (a common obsessive feature).

Why should he care, after all, at this late date? Was he concerned that her bad reputation would somehow rub off on him and thereby sully his standing? That hardly seems likely. Why can't he just let her live her own life?

The ghost *does* ask him to "step between her and her fighting soul" during his long discussion with her, but had it asked him to intervene with her in the first place? No. In fact, the ghost said:

> Let not the royal bed of Denmark be
> A couch for luxury and damned incest.
> But, howsoever thou pursuest this act,
> Taint not thy mind, nor let thy soul contrive
> Against thy mother aught: leave her to heaven
> And to those thorns that in her bosom lodge,
> To prick and sting her. (I, v, 89–95)

Hamlet nevertheless takes it upon himself to tell her to stop sleeping with Claudius, something that would be a moot point if he did what the ghost told him to do and dispatched Claudius to the grave! He seems to want his mother to do some of his work ("Let not the royal bed of Denmark be / A couch for luxury and damned incest") for him.

Three Stages in the Object-Relation

Can we understand Ophelia to be a little other for Hamlet? Something does happen regarding Ophelia, who had clearly been the object of Hamlet's affection at a certain point, he having written numerous love letters to her. We saw earlier that, in Lacan's view, after speaking with the ghost, something begins to evolve in his relationship to Ophelia: stage one in the object-relation, "estrangement" from the object (S6, p. 319). He stares at her for quite some time and yet is unable to recognize her or see her as he had seen her in prior times.

I will comment on stage two a bit further on, but let us jump directly to what Lacan calls stage three in the object-relation: competition with Laertes regarding the mourning of this object. Laertes (whom Hamlet is twice said by his uncle to envy [IV, vii, 84 and 117]) jumps into his sister's grave to kiss her one last time, and it is in imitation of this, and, indeed, in competition with Laertes' no-holds-barred lamentations over his sister (V, i, 285–301) that Hamlet is finally able, Lacan suggests, to reconstitute Ophelia as a loved object that he has lost. Lacan speaks here of "a reintegration of a" (S6, p. 322). Recall, once again, that it is the lost object that contains within itself or somehow harbors within itself minus phi, the imaginary phallus. He tells us that "The object is reconquered here only at the price of mourning and death" (p. 322).

"The backdrop," Lacan says,

> is this scene in which Hamlet suddenly sees the passionate relationship of a subject with an object, this relationship being manifested by someone else [Laertes]. This scene grabs him and offers him a prop by which his own relationship as a subject, $\cancel{S}$, with Ophelia—little object a, which had been rejected owing to the confusion or compounding of objects—is suddenly reestablished. And it is this suddenly reestablished level that is momentarily going to make a man of him (S6, pp. 288–9)

and allow him to wield the phallus.

It is only by mourning the loss of the imaginary phallus that Hamlet can finally come to grips with the symbolic phallus—a.k.a., the signifier of the lack in the Other. Hamlet explains that

the bravery of [Laertes'] grief did put me
Into a tow'ring passion. (V, ii, 89–90)

It would seem that it is this towering passion that somehow catapults Hamlet to the upper level of the Graph, allowing him to definitively mourn the loss of the object that incarnated all of his losses.[4]

Turning now to what Lacan designates as stage two, we encounter complications. How does one go from estrangement to mourning? Here is the passage that follows Lacan's discussion of the "estrangement" episode:

In Hamlet's case, it seems that after this episode [the "To be or not to be speech," after which Ophelia returns his letters to him (III, i, 110–12)] Ophelia has completely ceased to exist for him as a love object. "I did love you once," says Hamlet [III, i, 115]. [...]

In Hamlet's attitude toward Ophelia, we find a trace of the imbalance in the fantasized relationship that I mentioned earlier—the fantasy tilts toward the object, toward perversion. This is one of the features of their relationship. Another is that the object in question is no longer treated as she had been before—that is, as a woman.

To Hamlet, Ophelia becomes a bearer of children and of sins of all ilks. She is doomed to engender sinners and to then have to succumb to all sorts of calumny. She becomes the pure and simple medium for a form of life that is, in its essence, now condemned. In short, what happens at this moment is the destruction or loss of the object, which is *reintegrated into its narcissistic frame* [my emphasis].

To the subject, the object appears outside, as it were. The formulation that I provided earlier indicates to you what this object is equivalent to, what it takes the place of, and what cannot be given to the subject except

---

[4] Rivalry with Laertes as little *a* and mourning the loss of Ophelia as minus phi all rolled into one?

at the moment at which he literally sacrifices himself, at which he is no longer it himself, at which he rejects it with his whole being. This object is clearly no other than the phallus.

Yes, Ophelia is at that moment the phallus, the phallus qua signifying symbol of life, the phallus that the subject externalizes and rejects as such. This is the second stage of the relationship to the object.

We do not have much time left and so I hesitate to give you all the coordinates here. I will return to this. But the fact that this is what is involved—namely, a transformation of the formula [and from there heads toward fantasy [($\cancel{S} \lozenge a$) into] ($\cancel{S} \lozenge \varphi$) in the guise of rejection [*rejet*]—is demonstrated, once you realize it, by something that has nothing to do with the etymology of Ophelia's name. […]

The entire dialogue with Ophelia shows that woman is conceptualized here only as carrying the vital turgescence [or: turgidity] that must be cursed and stopped up. As semantic usage shows, "nunnery" could also at that time designate a brothel.

Secondly, the relationship between the phallus and the object is also designated by Hamlet's attitude toward Ophelia during the play scene. When his mother, who is also there, asks him to sit by her, he replies, "No, good mother. Here's metal more attractive" [III, ii, 105], and puts his head between Ophelia's legs, asking her explicitly, "Lady, shall I lie in your lap?" [107]. The phallic quality of the object of desire [*Le rapport phallique de l'objet du désir*] is clearly indicated here. (S6, pp. 320–1)

This passage is no walk in the park!

It seems to me that there is a slight contradiction here between the matheme that Lacan provides, ($\cancel{S} \lozenge \varphi$), which clearly contains the *imaginary* phallus (although not negativized, as it usually is; S6, p. 321), and his characterization of the phallus involved here as "signifying symbol of life." Nevertheless, I think he is not talking here about the phallus as a signifier, but rather as a symbol or sign—thus something that remains in the imaginary register. We might say that, like a sign, it signifies something to someone, that it means something to certain people, if not to everyone, rather than representing the subject to another signifier.

As an aside, I would mention that Jungians seem to believe that they can interpret symbols universally, that is, that symbols mean the same thing for everyone, which is totally different from the Lacanian use of signifiers. φ, the phallus as a "signifying symbol of life," is a sort of Jungian symbol here, one that signifies turgidity, potency, and reproductive capability to one and all.

This is what Ophelia becomes here. The imaginary phallus she contained within herself shows nakedly through. The ideal qualities of Woman with a capital W are stripped away. No longer a fantasized embodiment of Truth and Beauty, Woman becomes trash, a slut, a producer of sinners and garbage.[5]

Now what does it mean when Lacan says that "what happens at this moment is the destruction or loss of the object, which is reintegrated into its narcissistic frame"? What "narcissistic frame" is he talking about?

I would propose that the backdrop here is Lacan's theorization of the formation of the ideal ego and the ego-ideal, which occurs in various stages, and is informed by a film made by Arnold Lucius Gesell (1880–1961), a man who apparently knew nothing of Lacan's mirror stage. It was entitled *La découverte de soi devant le miroir* (*The Discovery of Oneself in Front of the Mirror*); it was shown by Lacan to his audience on May 19, 1953, when he gave a talk entitled "The Mirror Stage in Action," and he discussed it in Seminar I (S1, p. 168).

I won't go into his reformulation of the mirror stage in Seminar VIII now, as it is posterior to this specific seminar (and I have done so elsewhere).[6]

---

[5] If Hamlet can be said to have "womb envy," it would seem to be highly repressed!

[6] Yet it might be relevant to the way in which Lacan interprets how Hamlet accedes to the phallus here, it being only on the basis of the imaginary, whereas Seminar VIII provides a second moment to the mirror stage, which is symbolic and concerns the formation of the ego-ideal via the unary trait.

In Seminar VIII, Lacan (2015) hypothesizes—on the basis of a film showing footage of six- to 18-month-olds placed in front of a mirror as their parents stand nearby—that a child's mirror image becomes invested with libido and internalized due to *recognition* of the child by the parent, due, for example, to the parent's exclamation as a child looks at itself in the mirror, "Yes, Baby, that's you!" A child—as seen in this film—often turns its head away from the mirror image toward its parent to see the parent looking at the child looking at itself in the mirror, and the parent often provides a kind of confirmatory nod or approving gesture, if not an exclamation. This leads to what Lacan calls a validation or ratification (*entérinement*) of the mirror image.

The "parent's nod" serves as *ein einziger Zug* (a single trait, stroke, or characteristic), a term Freud uses in *Group Psychology and the Analysis of the Ego* (SE XVIII). This trait concerns the respect in which the parent approves of the child or finds the child to be lovable. The child identifies with or

What concerns us here is, I think, Lacan's interest in the fact that in the film a number of the infants who are placed naked in front of the mirror cover their genitalia with a hand. Lacan proposes that the ideal ego forms in such a way that what we might call the "offending part of the anatomy" is excluded from it. Those parts are not considered to be ideal, presumably by the infant's entourage, and they are not integrated into the ideal image of oneself that forms in this first phase of the mirror stage. They are not narcissistically invested, as it were, and are excluded from the narcissistic frame. The child cannot see itself as a whole if the genitalia are included. If they are excluded, a whole, totalizing image *can* come into being.

Consider what Lacan says in "Subversion of the Subject":

> the specular image is the channel taken by the transfusion of the body's libido toward the object. But insofar as a part remains preserved from this immersion, concentrating in itself the most intimate aspect of autoeroticism, its position as a "pointy extremity" in the form predisposes it to the fantasy of it falling off—in which its exclusion from the specular image is completed as is the prototype it constitutes for the world of objects. (*Écrits*, pp. 696–7)

I'm not suggesting that this is by any means transparent, but the general idea seems to be that subjects imagine that what protrudes can fall off or be lopped off, and this is crucial to our conception of objects in general.

---

brings into itself the external point or place from which it is seen as lovable by the parent, and thereby comes to see itself as it is seen by that parent. It begins to see itself as if it were itself in the parent's position, viewing the child from the outside.

This leads to the formation of what Freud calls the ego-ideal—the point at which one is viewed as worthwhile by the Other—which is what allows a sense of self to form. This *einziger Zug* (which Lacan eventually translates as "unary trait," his shorthand for it being S_1), as the core of the ego-ideal, is the anchoring point of the entire symbolic order, leading as it does to internalization of an outside position whereby one learns to see oneself as (one believes) others see one. The Other's approving gaze at oneself is brought inside, as it were, and one begins to view oneself approvingly as the Other views one (the Other's disapproving gaze will, of course, come into play as well).

The parent's approval or ratification here (S_1, the core of the ego-ideal) allows, in theory, for the *internalization* of the mirror image itself—that is, of the ideal ego—there being henceforward an ideal image or set of images that structure one's sense of self.

See my fuller discussion of the mirror stage in Chapter 5 of Fink (2016).

In what Lacan in Seminar VI calls "stage two" of the relation to the object, where the object is "reintegrated into its narcissistic frame," it seems that the genitalia return. They return so significantly that they destroy or contaminate all the ideal features the object had been endowed with before. In this case, they seem to be all that Hamlet can see in Ophelia. And he is thoroughly disgusted by it.

Curiously enough, they are not her genitalia, but rather some sort of phallic symbol. Let us note a curious contrast here between Gertrude and Ophelia: according to Lacan, Hamlet comes away from his long conversation with his mother, thinking her a "gaping cunt," whereas he supposedly sees Ophelia as the imaginary phallus and rejects her.

Alternatively, Lacan might mean that Ophelia herself is knocked off her symbolic pedestal here, and falls back into the imaginary framework of a—a', or m—$i(a)$. In that sense, she falls into the position of being a semblable for Hamlet, just as corrupt as he is. Since he is disgusted by himself, undoubtedly for multiple reasons, he has reason to be disgusted by her too.[7]

As Lacan puts it, in the "second stage" the object becomes the phallus—let us say here "the genitalia"—"that the subject externalizes and rejects" (S6, p. 321). Woman, as Truth and Beauty and all such ideal virtues, has crumbled to dust before Hamlet's eyes (or ears)… ("O most pernicious woman!" cries Hamlet upon hearing the news from the ghost; I, v, 112).

Whether we opt for the first or second of these interpretations of his meaning here, we might think of Lacan's "second stage" of the relation to the object as correlated in Freud's work with the stage of the Oedipus complex at which the young boy finally reckons with the fact that his mother continues to sleep with his father, and is not selflessly saving herself for him. She is unfaithful to him and thus a whore. As Freud puts it in *The Ego and the Id*, "Along with the demolition of the Oedipus complex, the boy's object-cathexis of his mother must be given up" (SE XIX, pp. 31–2).

---

[7] At the end of Seminar V, Lacan characterizes the m—$i(a)$ relation with the following sentence: *Tu es celui qui me tues*, "You are the one who 'yous' me," that is, who makes me into a "you," into someone; however, there is a homophony between the forged verb *tues* (to you someone) and kill. Hence: "You are the one who kills me"; S5, p. 446).

The question that arises is whether he can go beyond that disenchant-ment with his mother and move on, no longer projecting the powerful imaginary phallus onto her, no longer locating it in the object, but some-how raising it up from an imaginary symbol to the dignity of a signifier that he himself can wield: power wielded through knowledge, artistry, craftiness, moral righteousness, or money—it can take many forms. "It is to the degree to which he gives up his relationship to the [person who incarnates the imaginary] phallus that the subject can possess the infinity of objects that characterize the human world" (S6, p. 214).

In Freud's schematic picture of male development, this might seem to correspond to successful negotiation of the castration complex, which puts an end to the Oedipus complex.

Is this Lacan's stage three? Does Hamlet's competition with Laertes regarding the mourning of this object allow him access to the symbolic phallus? Lacan speaks of "a reintegration of [object] *a*" and tells us that:

> In this scene, the highest function of the object is in some sense traced out. The object is reconquered here only at the price of mourning and death. (S6, p. 322)

Can we simply say, hurrah, the signifier kills the thing? The phallic signifier kills off the object that contains minus phi? Is it when that object is reconstituted and successfully mourned that capital Phi, the phallus as a signifier, can come to the fore? Is the real lack in the world brought on by the death of Ophelia—who Hamlet perhaps intended to be his future queen—finally symbolized here? Is his attachment to queens overcome (he can sacrifice his queen in life's game of chess?) and he can finally accede to his desire (which is his father's desire that he kill Claudius, that justice be served)? I'll leave those as open questions.

The Headline Claims Revisited

We have arrived at a point in our discussion of *Hamlet* where some of Lacan's headline claims can be glossed. Regarding "the tragedy of *Hamlet* is the encounter with death," it might be said that it is the encounter with his father's death that confronts Hamlet with the lack in the Other, and the encounter with Ophelia's death that finally serves as the motor force for his accession to the signifier of the lack in the Other.

Regarding the claim that *Hamlet* is "the tragedy of desire" (pp. 249 and 306), we might propose that this is because Hamlet is forced to give up his desire for his mother and for Ophelia, and only accedes to his fully fledged desire when it is too late.

Desire is inextricably bound up with mourning (p. 345), as we have seen. What does he mourn? The loss of the reliable Other, and the loss of his belief in Woman as the embodiment of Beauty and Truth.

"The tragedy is founded on the subject's relationship to truth" insofar as Hamlet is forced to realize that there is no truth with a capital *T*, no Truth about the truth, as it were, but only "the moment of truth"—the moment at which he accedes to his desire and takes action, at which he puts his desire into action.

Hamlet, like the obsessive more generally, is always living on the Other's time, the Other's watch, not on his own. He always peaks too early or prepares for something when it is too late, never choosing to do something when the time is ripe for him but leaving it up to fate to decide when to act. "The time is out of joint" (I, v, 210). This is true right up to the end, where it is Death itself that calls the shots, determining that he has no time to declare to the world what has happened in the court of Denmark. He calls upon Horatio to "report me and my cause aright / To the unsatisfied" (V, ii, 371–2). "There's a divinity that shapes our ends, / Rough-hew them how we will" (V, ii, 12). In that sense, we might say he never overcomes his problematic relationship to time. He remains in the curious state where:

> If it be now, 'tis not to come;
> if it be not to come, it will be now;
> if it be not now, yet it will come. (V, ii, 234–6)

Consider the next headline: *Hamlet* is the play that, *par excellence*, juxtaposes knowledge and desire. This is because Hamlet must learn to act without having perfect or complete knowledge of what is going on or what the outcome will be. He has to trust in fate and act on his desire, come what may. Note that this is true for all of us: we cannot know in advance the exact outcome of our actions and of all the alternative actions we might take. Either we never put our desire into action or we learn to live with our structural lack of omniscience.

"What Hamlet is constantly dealing or grappling with is a desire which is far from being his own. As it is situated in the play, it is the desire, not *for* his mother, but *of* his mother—that is, it is his mother's desire" (S6, p. 280). The unconscious desire he is grappling with is his *interpretation* of his mother's desire. What he most profoundly and secretly wants is what he is convinced she wants. What is he convinced she wants? According to Lacan, she wants it all the time, and it doesn't matter with whom she gets it. Does he delay for so many months in order to let her have it?!

There are two wrinkles here:

1. In Seminar XIV, *The Logic of Fantasy*, Lacan repeats a claim he implicitly makes in Seminar VI: "Desire is its interpretation" (S14, p. 417). But in Seminar XIV he proposes that the definition of unconscious desire is "le *désir pas*," "I don't want it" (p. 417). What don't you want? What the Other wants. Unconscious desire is an interpretation of the Other's desire and a refusal thereof, a denial thereof. It would seem that I say I want what the Other wants, but unconsciously I don't.
2. Lacan claims that Hamlet's mother "is less desire than gluttony and even engulfment" (p. 300); thus Hamlet encountered "something from the real Other"—not his mother's desire, but her demand or jouissance.

Is his desire freed from her "gluttony" and "engulfment" by the end of the play? Food for thought …

9

Questions that Arise from Lacan's Reading of *Hamlet*

Did Lacan live up to his own criteria about how to read poetic works? Recall what he said when he critiqued analysts for simply trying to find confirmation for their own pre-existing concepts in works of art: "poetic creations generate psychological creations more than they reflect them." In other words, they give us something new. Did he find something new in *Hamlet*, or simply apply his existing categories to it?

Another question that grows out of Lacan's reading of *Hamlet*: we can ask each man (at least) whether the object of his desire continues to secretly or surreptitiously harbor within itself all the losses of jouissance associated with the imaginary phallus, or whether he has mourned its loss, gone beyond that stage, and come to grips with the symbolic phallus. It's a question that is more easily raised than answered.

And it is tantamount to asking to what degree we continue to locate our own castration within our partners. The flaws and failings we attribute to our partners are flaws and failings we encounter in ourselves, first and foremost. What, then, are we doing when we cleave to such partners? Are we loving our castration as we love ourselves (to adapt Freud's formulation that psychotics love their delusions as they love themselves)? Do we

© The Author(s), under exclusive license to Springer Nature Switzerland AG 2025
B. Fink, *Lacan on Desire*, The Palgrave Lacan Series,
https://doi.org/10.1007/978-3-031-76386-1_9

love and hate our castration, alternately drawing it close and pushing it away?

Does love, there, take the form of self-pity? Is tenderness displayed to the other a disguised way of pitying ourselves for our own loss? Lacan is not especially tender when it comes to tenderness! Consider what he says about it in Seminar XIV:

> We could label a facet of tenderness, and perhaps all of tenderness, with a formulation that would be pretty close to the following: tenderness is the pity it is suitable to have with respect to the inability [or: impotence, *impuissance*] to love. (S14, p. 234)

To take this a step further, we can ask if castration is ever complete. What would it mean for castration to be complete? Or to use a term Lacan uses more systematically starting in Seminar XI, for separation to be complete? Is it always a question of more or less? The later notion of the traversing of fantasy might suggest that castration and separation can be completed at a certain ideal point (S11, p. 273). Would that imply that by the end of the play, Hamlet has traversed his fantasy?!

And what about the case of women? Do they situate their own castration in their partner? Or do they experience themselves as the object that harbors and covers over their partner's castration? If so, they, too, will be stuck in a sense: loving him for his castration and desiring elsewhere. Lacan does suggest that what a woman loves in a man is his castration (see S18, p. 104; and S16, p. 28); that's not what she desires, but what she loves.

Does *Hamlet* have something to teach us about analytic interpretation? Consider the following passage (even if it is uttered by Polonius):

> See you now
> Your bait of falsehood take this carp of truth;
> And thus do we of wisdom and of reach,
> With windlasses [circuitous, artful courses] and with assays of bias,
> By indirections find directions out. (II, i, 70–73)

Gesturing Toward the Ethics Seminar, Seminar VII

Did Shakespeare contribute anything to Lacan's theory? Just for fun, I will end my discussion of *Hamlet* by juxtaposing two lines, one from *Hamlet*, and one from the very next Seminar Lacan was to give:

> "to thine own self be true" (I, iii, 84)
> don't "give up on your desire" (S7, pp. 319 and 321)[1]

At least twice in Seminar VI, Lacan discusses the ethics tradition, including hedonism, which contrasts the good as postulated by the majority of moral philosophy, with pleasure. It seems clear already in Seminar VI that Lacan intends to replace the ethics of the good with an ethics of desire, which is precisely what he does in Seminar VII.

And toward the end of Seminar VI, he proffers the following

> On the day of the Last Judgment, won't what we will be able to say about what we have done, in our unique existence, to *realize our desire* weigh as heavily as what we will have done along the lines—which does not refute it in the slightest, which does not counterbalance it in any way—of doing what is known as the good? (S6, p. 412; my emphasis)

By the following year, his conclusion will be that what we do to realize our desire weighs far more heavily in the balance than the supposed good. Hence his ethical principle: don't give up on your desire!

---

[1] The published English translation reads: "give ground relative to one's desire," a rather cumbersome formulation in my view.

Part IV

Major Configurations of Desire: Perversion, Obsession, Hysteria, and Phobia

10

Perversion

The last section of Seminar VI is largely devoted to articulating desire and fantasy in the various clinical structures. We will begin with perversion.

Some Lacanians curiously claim that perversion as a separate clinical structure disappears from Lacan's work at a certain point, although exactly at what point that is strikes me as unclear.

I would argue that Lacan is remarkably consistent throughout his work in taking voyeurism, exhibitionism, sadism, masochism, and fetishism to constitute separate clinical structures—separate from each other and separate from neurosis and psychosis—and that precise formulations regarding perversion appear in numerous Seminars, including I, VI, VIII, X, XI, XIV, XVI, XVIII, XIX, XX, XXI, XXII, XXIII, and perhaps others as well (often at the end of the Seminars). His papers on Sade and Gide in *Écrits* also attest to his attempt to articulate the specific nature of perversion. (This doesn't mean that different features of perversion aren't emphasized from one Seminar to the next, or that the account of perversion in Seminar XVI doesn't at times contradict the accounts in Seminars VI and X.)

Lacan repeatedly stresses that "perverse fantasies are not perversion proper" (S6, p. 454) and criticizes numerous writers for being unable to

© The Author(s), under exclusive license to Springer Nature Switzerland AG 2025   **119**
B. Fink, *Lacan on Desire*, The Palgrave Lacan Series,
https://doi.org/10.1007/978-3-031-76386-1_10

distinguish between them; see, for example, his comments regarding the French authors of an article in the *International Journal of Psychoanalysis*, who apparently threw up their hands, saying they could see no difference. One rather clear distinction between neurosis and perversion that Lacan draws is that, whereas the neurotic cannot accede to or reach the object, the pervert can (p. 455). And the pervert disappears in the process in an experience of jouissance.

The Exhibitionist

Consider, first, the exhibitionist. He does not go to nude beaches, nudist colonies, or sex clubs where his exposed genitalia will be easily accepted by his entourage. Instead, he spends his time violating other people's sense of propriety and modesty by exposing himself to those he believes likely to be shocked by his unexpected flashing. To violate them in this way is to call forth their division as subjects: it is to call forth in them *disgust*, which is indicative of repressed desire. This brings out the split between their desire to see and their moral repugnance, or between the unconscious and the ego (or superego). Lacan does not emphasize in Seminar VI the arousal of anxiety in the viewer sought by the exhibitionist as he does in Seminar X, *Anxiety*, but it is already suggested here in the notion that the viewer is *disturbed* at the level of modesty or shame, which is an indicator or sign of unconscious desire.

The viewer's unconscious desire to see is precisely what the exhibitionist lives to see. To flash in front of someone who is blasé, and indeed comments that she's "seen better"—as was reported to me by someone I once supervised in Pittsburgh—deflates him, whereas someone who screams delights him. And he takes the shocked look, and the sharp taking in of breath or scream, as having struck a chord in his viewer. Lacan refers to this as the kind of "complicity" on the viewer's part that the exhibitionist is seeking.

To orchestrate such complicity requires a whole staging process or scenario on the exhibitionist's part that involves a slit: the opening up of a raincoat or the fly of his pants. And this must occur in a public place where there is some danger of being caught and arrested. The more danger the better! The law is thus integrally woven into the backdrop of this scenario, insofar as it is necessarily violated. I suspect that there can be no such thing as exhibitionism in countries where such flashing is not prohibited.

The exhibitionist's scenario thus always requires prohibition and the possibility of getting caught and punished. He wants an anxious sign of a girl's unconscious desire, and yet simultaneously wants the police (the big daddy) to be close enough to catch him. Lacan does not explore the pervert's relation to the law in Seminar VI, merely mentioning the importance of "danger" in the perverse scenario, but clinical experience shows that many exhibitionists express relief and pleasure when they are caught. They feel they deserve to be punished for their actions, realizing they are asking for it. While they are exhibiting, they are flaunting the law, thumbing their noses at it, but they seem to want to test it, to bring it into the picture.

Their question seems to be: "Will I actually be punished (by daddy) for provoking or arousing my mother's desire?" (We might imagine a toddler in a diaper as it is being removed.) When we consider cases closely, we usually find little to no prohibiting in the household the exhibitionist grew up in: no one, and certainly not the pervert's father, meted out punishment. Lip service may have been given to condemning bad behavior, but the latter was tacitly excused by mom with a "wink, wink"—"we won't tell your father about that." When exhibitionists are not caught, they tend to escalate and exhibit themselves in ever more public places where they are increasingly likely to be apprehended.

The pervert's fantasy is sometimes depicted as $a \longrightarrow \math{S}$ (not in Seminar VI, of course), implying, in the exhibitionist's case, that he sees himself as bringing out the split in the subject before whom he exposes himself, as the cause of the viewer's discomfort and anxiety. He is not the one who is a split subject—the other person is. Castration is thus cast upon the other.

The Voyeur

We find much the same thing in voyeurism as in exhibitionism. Lacan tells us that the slit is, again, absolutely crucial here: the voyeur looks through a little opening between curtains, between boards in a fence, or a door that is already ajar or that he cracks open. Like the exhibitionist, he is in some sense reduced to the slit in this scenario. And like the exhibitionist, he is looking for some kind of complicity in the other party, the woman he observes, seeking to detect some sort of sign, or at least, imagining a sign that she is "offering herself up to his [scopic] jouissance" (S6, p. 418), offering herself up to be seen, and indeed enjoying the idea that she might be seen by an invisible other. The voyeur does not go to a nude beach or a strip club to look at more or less naked women, because the women at such places are obviously offering themselves up to be seen; there is nothing unconscious about that offer in their cases, and no sense of impropriety that is at stake.

Nor is there anything prohibited about him being there and looking. The voyeur believes that what he is doing should *not* be permitted and that he should be punished for it. Moreover, there is evidence that he does not want to see the woman's genitals (i.e., the slit); anything but! He wants to glimpse her supposedly secret enjoyment of being seen, which is perhaps also a bit uncomfortable to her, giving rise to some anxiety in her—especially if she hears some rustling in the bushes, some noise he "inadvertently" makes, signaling that someone is there, watching.

He sees himself as the implicit cause (he being the potential viewer) of her desire to be seen and of her discomfort with that same desire while "unwittingly" exhibiting herself.

The Pervert Goes Straight for Jouissance Whereas the Neurotic Avoids It

Lacan tells us that the slit (through which he looks or exposes himself) gives the pervert access to the Other's desire (S6, p. 420), opening him up "to a desire other than his own" (p. 423). Time stops here; it is suspended.

The subject fades and disappears when faced with the Other's desire. This is where the pervert experiences jouissance; jouissance happens for him when he is "at [the] mercy" of the Other's desire (p. 424). At that point he has "no recourse" (p. 425), he is helpless. And he repeats this moment of helplessness again and again. For him, it is a *tolerable* form of jouissance, whereas such helplessness is in no way tolerable to the neurotic who avoids it like the plague. The neurotic is terrified by the Other's desire (p. 466) and defends against it at any cost. The neurotic's "desire is a defense" against the Other's desire (p. 428).[1]

Whereas the pervert goes straight for the jouissance of a kind of subjective annihilation when faced with the Other's desire, the neurotic avoids it. As Lacan puts it regarding hysterics, they "derive jouissance from blocking" the Other's desire (S6, p. 427). And as he puts it regarding phobia, which he considers to be the most radical form of neurosis, the phobic creates a phobia in order to protect against the encounter with the Other's desire, as manifested in the Other's *manque à être*—that is, the Other's wanting something or lacking in something. (This perhaps explains, at least in part, his claim in Seminar XIV that the definition of unconscious desire is "le *désir pas*," "I don't want it"? What don't you want? What the Other wants [S14, p. 417].)

For neurotics, the encounter with the Other's desire is always traumatic, and they find ways to grapple with it. The Other's desire "absorbs" the subject and leaves him or her no recourse. Phobia is the erection of an object/signifier to protect one from the Other's desire, which is always traumatic.[2]

Neurotics form symptoms that are precisely designed to sustain their presence as subjects when faced with the Other's desire. Neurotic symptoms are thus all structured like phobias in the sense that they are all

---

[1] This should undoubtedly be qualified: the neurotic consciously defends against the Other's desire, while unconsciously making the Other's desire his or her own.

Women rarely, if ever, are truly perverse, structurally speaking: "Men have, at least apparently, the privilege of occupying the major perverse positions" (Lacan, S14, p. 382).

[2] Regarding Hans, Lacan says that his mother is "prey to a lack" related to the phallus, which he doesn't have (S6, pp. 425–6). The phallic object receives a function from the symbolic order, a function that allows it to be used "as an arm at the phobic outpost, an arm against the threat of desire's disappearance"—i.e., the disappearance of the subject in the Other—"and the role of a fetish in perverse structure, as the absolute condition of desire" (*Écrits*, p. 571).

designed to block something coming from or detected in the Other that is unbearable and to prevent the subject from fading or disappearing altogether in the encounter.

Perversion seeks a direct encounter with jouissance, whereas neurosis is a defense against jouissance. The neurotic may well fantasize about having such a direct encounter with jouissance, but should a situation present itself where he could go for it, he tends to run the other way, fall apart, or have a ("nervous") breakdown.

The pervert feels he *is* the phallus—as he was for his mother, the desiring Other, whose desire he can access in the scenario—and simultaneously that he *has* the phallus at his disposal. This is the pervert's "both/and logic" (as I call it [see Chapter 9 in Fink 2014a]; cf. S6, p. 464).[3]

The obsessive, on the other hand, is conscious of *not* being the phallus, but perhaps believes he has it and might someday be able to wield it. Yet he still secretly—that is unconsciously—believes he *is* it. Thus in neurosis, these beliefs (regarding being and having) are held at different levels (conscious and unconscious), whereas in perversion they are held at one and the same level (Freud called this "the splitting of the ego" in which two contradictory ideas are held side by side, like "my mother has a penis" and "my mother does not have a penis").

In neurosis, the wish to be and remain the phallus, as opposed to wielding it, leads to all kinds of avoidance scenarios, the kind we see, for example, very often in obsession where the obsessive "elects a substitute" for himself (S6, p. 452). For example, he is in love with a specific woman, but rather than pursuing her, which might require him to assume possession of the phallus, he gets his best friend interested in her. Once she and his best friend are involved, he continues to imagine that she secretly admires him more than his best friend, realizing that he is the far more valuable object than his friend is. But he never has to put himself to the test. He doesn't have it; "it is an other who has it" (p. 451).

Lacan provides a rather curious variation on the matheme for fantasy in such cases:

---

[3] The Other's desire as phallus, with which he identifies, is everything at that moment, the subject nothing. She has the phallus in the form of her desire, and he, being the apple of her eye, *is* the phallus for her. He can have it via the partner (S6, p. 465).

$$\Phi \lozenge i(a)$$

Here we see that the subject is identified with the phallus (which is oddly barred on page 452, but not on page 465) and the object is his alter ego—in this case, his best friend.

In the case of hysteria, this alter ego is the other woman that the hysteric introduces into the couple, trying to detect a desire on her partner's part for this other woman, and failing that, inciting a desire for the other woman in him by talking about her constantly or inviting her over. Why would she do so? Presumably in order to have the other woman be the fallen object with which her partner obtains jouissance, while she remains the ideal, pristine Phallus with a capital P, unsullied by sex.

11

The Fundamental Fantasy

The subject [is] represented [in fantasy] at the very moment of his disappearance.
—Lacan (S6, p. 415)

[Fantasy is] the relationship between the subject's desire and … the Other's desire, […] between the subject's desire and what the Other desires.
—Lacan (S6, p. 422)

What can we glean about the fundamental fantasy from Seminar VI? Many things, of course, but first and foremost the idea that fantasy appears owing to the failure to desire, the non-assumption of one's desire (S6, p. 414). The implicit claim here is that when we really and truly desire, we dissipate fantasy, we have no need for fantasy. This intersects with what we say in everyday discourse about fantasy when we say that so and so is stuck in a fantasy world, or is a dreamer or a daydreamer, and never gets around to actually doing anything to realize his or her dreams and fantasies.

The subject is represented in fantasy "at the very moment of his disappearance" from full-fledged desire. When desire is in play, when desire is in motion, there is no need for fantasy.

© The Author(s), under exclusive license to Springer Nature Switzerland AG 2025
B. Fink, *Lacan on Desire*, The Palgrave Lacan Series,
https://doi.org/10.1007/978-3-031-76386-1_11

According to Lacan, fantasy operates when the subject "falters … in his certainty as a subject," "in his designation as a subject" (S6, p. 367)—that is, when the subject can't name himself (p. 413), when he can't identify himself as the subject of his own discourse" (p. 367) and say who and what he is. Recall that Hamlet is unable to identify himself until the end of the play, when he can finally say, "I, Hamlet the Dane."[1] (We shall return to this further on.)

Object *a* comes into play here, being "defined first of all as the prop the subject gives himself inasmuch as he falters" (S6, p. 366). We might almost speculate here that a subject has no need for object *a* as a prop when he or she comes into his or her own as a desiring subject (see Fig. 11.1). Indeed, Lacan seems to suggest that when one is able to name oneself, one loses object *a*, one castrates oneself (p. 372). On the contrary, the unconscious is where the subject cannot name himself, cannot say who or where he is (p. 378).

Recall that Lacan has not yet formulated his later notion of traversing fantasy, but there are hints in that direction here, suggesting not simply a reconfiguration of fantasy, but that one has no further need for it whatsoever once one has assumed, taken on, or owned and acted on one's own desire (becoming one's own cause of desire).

Moving ever further in the direction of conceptualizing object *a* differently, Lacan provides two different stages in the development of fantasy, which he defines as "the relationship between the subject's desire and [...] the Other's desire" (S6, p. 422). In stage one, object *a* takes the form of

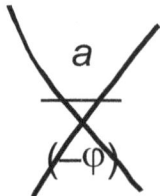

Fig. 11.1 The desiring subject has no further need to prop himself up with object *a*

---

[1] Yet Lacan also says that the subject's desire is "propped up" by fantasy…. Perhaps it is the subject, not the subject's desire, that is "propped up" by fantasy.

"the other's image [which] serves to prop up the subject." In stage two, we find "the more complex structure known as fantasy," wherein little *a* is the Other's desire. We see here a shift from the little other as desire or from the little other's desire to the Other with a capital *O* as desire or to the desire of the Other with a capital *O*.

We should make it a habit as we read Lacan's work to try out in our heads two different translations for *le désir de l'Autre*: the Other's desire and "what the Other desires." Here we might understand the idea that little *a* is the Other's desire as "little *a* is what the Other desires" or "little *a* is the object that the Other desires." This paves the way for a number of different readings of the fundamental fantasy: the subject is confronted with the Other's desire, a desire which is at the crux of the subject's own desire; the subject is confronted with an object, or something more abstract, an X, an unknown, that the Other wants, leading the subject's own desire to mimic the Other's desire as it pursues one object after another, or pursue that very abstract thing known in psychoanalysis as the Phallus, which may be found momentarily in multiple objects (giving rise to what I once referred to as the "wild goose chase known as desire").[2]

It is important to stress here that, even if the subject's desire is the Other's desire (S6, p. 485), the Other's desire is not something that is directly known to the subject, even if the Other has striven to explicitly articulate it in words. The Other's desire is always something that has to be interpreted by the subject. Let's say a child's mother says she wants excitement, adventure, and to be swept off her feet—all of those are pretty vague to a child and call for interpretation!

And the child can always wonder, "Mom is saying that she wants X, but is that really true? Wouldn't she prefer Y? Or maybe that is not what she wants at all, for it doesn't seem to be what she pursues"; or "Maybe she's just saying that it's okay if I back out of a competition I have signed up for, but she really wants me to go and do my best."

---

[2] See Fink (1991, p. 75). Cf. Lacan's assertion that "little *a* is the Other's desire" (or: "little *a* is what the Other desires") (S6 p. 420); see, also, his claim that the object of desire is the Other's desire (p. 478). We try to fill the lack in ourselves with the Other's desire for us.

What we take to be the Other's desire is thus never anything more than our interpretation of what the Other wants. The Other's desire is an "enigma" (S6, p. 480) and can only be interpreted. Hamlet, Lacan claims, "interprets everything the Other [e.g., Gertrude] articulates about her most profound intention, and about her good or bad faith" (p. 376).[3]

Now, insofar as the subject's desire is the Other's desire, the subject's desire is an interpretation of the Other's desire. Hence

desire (i.e., the subject's desire)
is the subject's own interpretation (of the Other's desire)

Desire is, thus, in a sense, its own interpretation: an interpretation itself and of itself.

This leads Lacan to a whole series of Hegelian-sounding formulations, or circular-sounding definitions.

- The Phallus is the signifier of desire.
- The Phallus is "the signifier of the desire for desire" (S6, p. 479)—in other words, the signifier of the subject's desire for the Other to desire him or her, or the signifier of the subject's desire for what the Other desires.
- The Phallus is the signifier of the Other's desire (S6, pp. 466 and elsewhere).

These give rise to the apparent conclusion that "desire has no other object than the signifier [Φ] of its recognition" (S6, pp. 478–9), suggesting that desire strives to be recognized; that this recognition takes the form of a signifier, Φ; and that this recognition is more important to

---

[3] At the end of Seminar V, Lacan characterizes the Other as both the locus of speech and "as a being of flesh and blood at whose mercy we are for the satisfaction of our demand," and "about whom we do not know how she receives [or: welcomes, *accueille*] our demand" (S5, p. 451).

desire than satisfaction is.[4] Recognition by whom, we might ask! The subject herself?

This may well remind us of what Lacan said about desire in dreams—that it is content with its own appearance or coming into being in the dream. It is, in a sense, satisfied simply by manifesting itself in a dream, as I said earlier. Whereas Freud tries to determine what specific desire is actually fulfilled in the unfolding of the dream, Lacan seems to emphasize the simple appearance of the desire in the dream, that appearance bringing its own satisfaction with it.

The difficulty of interpreting the Other's desire, of grappling with Φ, seems to be eluded by the pervert, according to Lacan, who, instead of interpreting the Other's desire qua symbolic phallus, "identifies with the imaginary form of the phallus" (S6, pp. 466–7). This clearly reflects a problem with regard to castration, which Lacan defines here (p. 367) as involving "the pure function of a signifier": castration involves raising up something real—presumably, the penis as a biological organ, and perhaps we should add here, too, the clitoris as a biological organ, or as imagined by the subject as something that can fall off or be cut off—to the pure function of a signifier. (On page 369 he says that it is "raised … to the function of a symbol.") Hamlet is presumably able to do so by the end of the play, but the pervert cannot do so.[5]

Note, in any case, the language used here: the raising up of something, for in Seminar VII we are going to see an object raised up to the dignity of the Thing, *das Ding*.

---

[4] Women, he says, don't demand satisfaction but instead demand to have what they don't have: desire/the phallus (S6, p. 447).

[5] At the end of Seminar V, Lacan even went so far as to refer to the phallus as the signifier of death (S5, p. 439), insofar as it is the elective part of the body associated with bringing life—associated as it is with life-giving potency—but also a symbol of the recognition by human beings that we will die someday, the recognition of death being possible only owing to language and thus not being found in other species. Lacan here considers that it is the phallus that receives the signification of death because of that, death of the individual in mammals being intimately connected with sexual reproduction (as opposed to asexual reproduction in certain other species).

The Sublation of Loss

This notion of raising up might also be understood to signal a parting of the ways in psychoanalytic practice. Certain schools, endorsing the notion that patients have suffered all kinds of losses, the ones Lacan associates with $-\varphi$, have developed an approach which purports to *compensate patients for those losses*. How? By re-mothering or reparenting them, by serving them as better parents than the ones they'd had growing up, and in that way turning that minus into a plus $(+\varphi)$, as it were, or at least zeroing it out $(-\varphi + \varphi = 0)$.

By way of contrast, Lacan's view is that *losses are inevitable and irreversible*, and they must be mourned. We mustn't spend our whole lives complaining that we've been gypped and trying to get back what we feel we've lost out on. Now, once those losses are recognized for what they are and mourned, they can be sublimated or sublated in a sense, transmogrified with the coming to the fore of the phallic signifier, the Phallus with a capital *P*, symbolized by the matheme Φ. This is a forward-looking, as opposed to a backward-looking project. Rather than regressing to childhood to repair all the "damage" that was done, there is a push toward the recognition that what was, simply was what it was, it had to be that way (there is no point whining "If only things had been different...."); and a push toward the symbolization of something that can move things forward.

What does a desire that is no longer fixated on $-\varphi$ look like? It would seem to be detached from all the little others to whom one has continued to look for love, care, understanding, solace, or pity; and to be detached from all the Others whose desires one has attempted to decipher and either embrace or block, imitate or flee, emulate or transgress, satisfy or frustrate. It would seem to be a sort of utopian desire, insofar as it is theorized to be free from all reliance upon others, free from all influence by others of whatever sort, little or big. The X or unknown of their desire no longer seems to matter compared to the Φ at the core of the subject's now "traversed desire," so to speak.

We get glimpses of such a desire at the end of certain analyses, where we see that the analysand no longer cares what other people think of his or her pursuits and goals, whether they be parents, partners, friends, or even the analyst. The analysand does things simply because he or she wants to, asking no one for permission, approval, or validation. They may be artistic, musical, athletic, commercial, intellectual, or any other sorts of pursuits. What is unique about them is that they are not engaged in to win love from anyone—whether specific people or from some abstract adoring public—but simply because they are of interest to and satisfying to the subject.

This may well strike us as redolent of the "acephalous" (S11, pp. 181 and 184, where it is rendered as "headless") subject who headlessly "lives out the drive" (p. 273) described by Lacan in Seminar XI, and of what he begins to call the "subject of jouissance" in Seminar XVI (see, for example, p. 119). Initially stuck at the level of demand—the child's demands addressed to the Other and the Other's demands of the child—then at the level of desire for the Other and of the Other's desire, we perhaps see here a pursuit of satisfaction that was inhibited hitherto. We might see in this a move from the imaginary, to the symbolic, and on to the real of satisfaction.

We might speculate here that, insofar as the "mainspring of neurosis is not to want the Other to be castrated" (S6, p. 229), the end of analysis coincides with an acceptance of the Other's castration. Φ is, after all, the signifier of the lack in the Other. It can thus only come to the fore with the recognition of the Other's lack, of the Other's castration.

This perhaps allows one's own losses to be re-signified as the Other's losses or failings: the losses I suffered were as they were because of the Other's failings, inadequate knowledge, insufficient kindness, tortured or faltering desire. Is acceptance of the Other's castration tantamount to acceptance of one's own?

Note that we see one more development regarding object a in Seminar VI that seems to bring us closer to object a as the cause of desire: on page 479, little a is characterized as a "residue" or "remainder."

Fluctuating Formulas
of the Fundamental Fantasy

Although most people are familiar with the usual formula for fantasy, $\cancel{S}\lozenge a$, Lacan provides quite a few variations on it in the course of his work. In "Subversion of the Subject," written only about a year after the end of Seminar VI, he tells us that $(-\varphi)$, the "imaginary function of castration," is situated in neurosis under the barred subject:

$$\frac{\cancel{S} \; \lozenge \; a}{(-\varphi)}$$

This would seem to contradict what he says in Seminar VI. He also suggests in "Subversion of the Subject" that $(-\varphi)$ can be situated under either term, and even implies that when it is situated under a (or $i(a)$) the fundamental fantasy is non-neurotic (he refers there to Alcibiades' [perverse?] desire for Socrates in Plato's *Symposium*; see *Écrits*, pp. 699–700).

$$\cancel{S} \lozenge \frac{i(a)}{(-\varphi)}$$

How might we understand the formula when minus phi is located under the subject? As Lacan repeatedly tells us, the object takes on so much value, so much importance, in fantasy that it eclipses the subject.[6]

One of my analysands told me that he feels overwhelmed and annihilated by every woman he even begins to talk with. About one of them, he said, "She eclipses me." A moment later he added, "She has moved into my head." He is someone whose own desire immediately fades in the presence of a woman's desire; he no longer knows what he wants, and can only orient himself in relation to what he believes the woman wants.

---

[6] We might say that the object here is what divides or castrates the subject, taking something precious away from him, and that the subject develops a very complex relationship with that object. This relationship includes being joined to it, separated from it, enveloped by it, a mere extension of it, and so on (*Écrits*, p. 542 n. 17). The fantasized relationship to it brings with it, instead of a feeling of emptiness or loss, a sense of fullness or completeness.

And what he believes she wants is, not unsurprisingly, based on what she explicitly demands. In this sense, we can hypothesize that for him fantasy is reduced to the relationship to the Other's demand, because it is unbearable to him to be in the presence of the Other's desire. Here we have $(\not{S} \lozenge D)$ instead of $(\not{S} \lozenge a)$.

By extension, this implies that he himself is the one who contains minus phi: to him, the female Other is complete, not castrated, not associated with any sort of lost jouissance. He is nothing, she is everything.

Formulas for Hysteria and Obsession

Desire is always elsewhere.

A year after giving his paper "Subversion of the Subject," Lacan provides specific formulas for fantasy in hysteria and obsession in Seminar VIII. Hysteria is written as follows (S8, p. 246):

$$\frac{a}{(-\varphi)} \; \lozenge \; A$$

The hysterical subject is said there to put herself in the place of the object in relation to the Other. In the case of Dora, Dora identifies with Herr K as little a and relates to Frau K as capital A. We might try to understand this by proposing that Herr K somehow harbors Dora's castration $(-\varphi)$ within himself in that scenario (he lacks Frau K's love like Dora does, Frau K's love being, as it turns out, more loyally directed to Dora's father than to Herr K or Dora; recall that Frau K rats Dora out to Dora's father!).

In the same Seminar, obsession is written as follows (S8, p. 250):

$$\not{A} \; \lozenge \; \varphi \, (a, \, a', \, a'', \, a''', \, \ldots)$$

There Lacan tells us that it is φ, the "imaginary function of castration," that renders all objects $(a, \, a', \, a'', \, a''', \, \ldots)$ of the obsessive's desire equivalent. Imaginary castration serves a function here akin to that of mathematical functions, like $f(x)$, in which the different objects are subjected to the same function when put in the place of the variable, x. Each new object embodies or incarnates all of the subject's losses.

$$\frac{a}{-\varphi}, \frac{a'}{-\varphi}, \frac{a''}{-\varphi}$$

The obsessive subject is purportedly written $\cancel{A}$ here because he "is never where he seems to designate himself."[7]

Note that hysteria and obsession receive commentary in every one of Lacan's Seminars!

Let us remark here that, given that each partner to a relationship has his or her own fundamental fantasy that mediates relations with the Other's desire, there can be no direct relationship between partners, no subject-to-subject relationship. In other words, Lacan's implicit claim here, which will be rendered very explicit later, is that there's no such thing as a sexual relationship. For desire is attached not to a real object—that is, not to an actual living, breathing person—but rather to a fantasy (S6, p. 19).

Let me point out that I know of no place in Lacan's work where he provides a formula or matheme of the psychotic's fantasy. This, I believe, implies that there is no desire or fantasy structure, strictly speaking, in psychosis, because there is no divided subject there.

---

[7] Note also the different "Φ functions" Lacan provides for hysteria and obsession in another context: "The Φ function of the lost signifier, to which the subject sacrifices his phallus, the form Φ(*a*) of male desire, $\cancel{A}\varphi$ of woman's desire ..." (*Écrits*, p. 572). In Seminar VI (p. 452), Lacan provides a still earlier formula for all of neurosis; he says that neurotics devote themselves to trying to satisfy all of the Other's demands at the expense of their own desire: $\cancel{S}\Diamond a$ is transformed into $\phi\Diamond i(a)$, the latter designating the "barred phallus" in the presence of an object of desire—the object here being the image of the imaginary other or ego. This formulation was no doubt a forerunner to that found in the *Écrits*: $\cancel{S}\Diamond D$. There Lacan says that the neurotic confuses "the Other's lack with the Other's demand. [T]he Other's demand takes on the function of the object in the neurotic's fantasy" (*Écrits*, p. 698).

In Seminar V, Lacan says that the obsessive destroys or cancels out (*annule*, S5, p. 458) the Other's desire, and has to stay at a certain distance from his own desire in order for it to continue to exist (p. 443), "in order for him not to be destroyed" (p. 459). Yet he tries to preserve the Other simultaneously, as his own existence is conditional upon the Other's existence. "If he actually managed to cancel out the Other, he could no longer exist as a subject" (p. 459).

Note that in Lacan's later work, $-\varphi$ still takes on the meaning of a loss (or minus) of jouissance that is positivized, as it were, in object *a* (see, for example, Lacan 1968, p. 23).

12

Conclusions

On Lacan's Polyvalent Mathemes

Virtually all of Lacan's mathemes have multiple meanings, and they tend to acquire ever more meanings as his Seminars proceed. Here is a list of almost everything he says in Seminar VI about what S (Ⱥ) and (𝔰◊D) designate:

- S (Ⱥ): it is the message from the unconscious (S6, p. 343), "the signifier given by the Other"; "the unconscious message"; "the signifier that is missing at the level of the Other"; "there is no Other of the Other"; "the Other's signifierness"; "the castration complex" (p. 466).
- (𝔰◊D): it is "the level of the code or law" (S6, p. 286); "the code of discourse"; "the code at the level of the unconscious"; "the confrontation between the barred subject and demand, capital D"; the location of all of object relations theory: "*What are known as object relations are, in fact, always relations between the subject and, not objects, as people say, but rather signifiers of demand*; and these relations arise especially at the specific moment called "the fading of the subject" (p. 311, my emphasis). "The subject's relation to his own demand" (p. 284); and since every demand is a demand for love, it is the subject's relation to his

© The Author(s), under exclusive license to Springer Nature Switzerland AG 2025
B. Fink, *Lacan on Desire*, The Palgrave Lacan Series,
https://doi.org/10.1007/978-3-031-76386-1_12

own demand for love (which, like desire, is crushed by masturbatory jouissance; p. 433). ($◊D) only comes into play in psychoanalysis where one deciphers the unconscious chain (upper horizontal line in the Graph of Desire) (pp. 394–5). ($◊D) is perhaps never once mentioned in Seminar VI as the matheme of the drive.[1]

A question I would raise here is: of what value is it to attribute so many different meanings to one and the same matheme or concept? We end up with a situation in which it seems we must assume that all these different definitions are identical in some way, or all somehow amount to the same thing. If they are different, why write them with the same symbol or give them the same name? The condensation of meaning or constellations of meanings certainly lead to a great deal of confusion in Lacan's work, and many of his students obviously complained to him that they did not understand what his symbols meant. Let me use as an example the lozenge or diamond in the formulas of fantasy and the drive. Here are some of the things that Lacan says about it in the course of his teaching and writing:

When the lozenge (◊) between the subject and object is first introduced in fantasy, Lacan says that the lozenge "simply implies [...] that everything that is at stake here is commanded by the quadratic relation [...] which states that there is no conceivable barred subject [...] that is not sustained by the ternary relation A a' a (S5, p. 297). In other words, the lozenge (*poinçon*) stands for the fact that each subject is characterized by the whole of the L Schema (see Fig. 5.1), by all four vertices of it involving imaginary and symbolic axes (but not a as real). He repeats this further on: "the lozenge ... is the same thing as the square of a much older fundamental schema [of mine]" (p. 415).

This is obviously but an early sketch, for just a few months later Lacan writes, in a footnote to "Direction of the Treatment," that "The sign ◊ registers the relations envelopment-development-conjunction-disjunction"

---

[1] Regarding the drive, let me indicate that Lacan comments at the end of Seminar V on the translation of Freud's *Trieb*, which he says, would be better translated with the scientific term "tropism, designating certain irresistible attractions, considered to be irreducible to chemical/physical attraction, that are found in animal behavior"; he also suggests the term *attirance*, "attraction" (S5, p. 453).

(*Écrits*, p. 542 n. 17). But the L Schema is still centrally involved in Lacan's diagrams of Sadean fantasy in "Kant with Sade," written in 1962 (*Écrits*, pp. 774 and 778). Nevertheless, in Seminar XI, *The Four Fundamental Concepts of Psychoanalysis* (1964), he indicates that the lozenge can be understood as referring to the operations of union and intersection in set theory and the psychoanalytic operations of alienation and separation.

In a word, this lozenge just keeps accumulating new meanings!

In the latter case, the one involving alienation and separation, Lacan was obviously not thinking of the symbols for those two logical or set theory operations when he first proposed the lozenge, but noticed that divided in half horizontally, it includes both of them. Similarly, he once mentioned that divided in half vertically it includes the symbols for greater than and less than, both of which he was happy to read into the symbol.

What are we to make of that? I will leave that as an open question here.

Capital Phi and Minus Phi

Let me end by saying a few words about what I feel is of value in the distinction between minus phi and capital Phi. Minus phi refers to all the losses we enumerated in Chap. 3 and regarding Hamlet:

$$\frac{-\varphi}{\text{loss of jouissance}}$$

alienation

Hamlet losses (father, mother, Ophelia, and throne)

The subject is lacking in jouissance and lacking in being. The object, *a*, is the only being there is. It is the being that I don't have; it is what I don't have.

Capital Phi, on the other hand, has to do with desire:

$$\frac{\Phi}{\begin{matrix}\text{I have a sense I know what my desire is,}\\ \text{and feel I can pursue it.}\\ \text{I feel I know who I am: (``I, Hamlet the Dane.'')}\\ \text{I am = being}\end{matrix}}$$

The goal is to arrive at a point at which one leaves minus phi behind, capital Phi taking center stage:

$$\frac{\Phi}{-\varphi}$$

Afterword

Lacan's comments on knowledge involve a very broad perspective, which is centered, for the most part, around the question of certainty—that is, of what guarantees the correctness and completeness of our knowledge. He reminds us that, in former times, God was considered to be the guarantor of knowledge about the world and of ethics—that is, of how the world works and of everything we should and should not do. Even in more recent times, someone like Einstein could attribute to God knowledge of the laws of physics. Other people would use the term "Nature" instead of "God," and claim that nature must know Newton's laws in order for things to proceed the way that they do, for the planets to revolve as they do, and so on. ("In discovering knowledge, we conceptualize it […] as already organized somewhere"; S6, p. 243.)

In an age where many fewer people believe in God, and thus believe that God can serve as the guarantor of our knowledge about the world, people, and ethics, another solution was found, a solution that continues to have an impact even today. Hegel came up with the idea of the inevitable and continual perfecting of man's knowledge, the idea being that, even though we don't have absolute knowledge now, we are clearly headed in the right direction and will inevitably get there. The guarantee that what we believe is correct is coming soon to a theater near you!

© The Author(s), under exclusive license to Springer Nature Switzerland AG 2025   **141**
B. Fink, *Lacan on Desire*, The Palgrave Lacan Series,
https://doi.org/10.1007/978-3-031-76386-1

The idea of absolute knowledge—or of its "absolutizability"—is thus preserved. Although few people probably continue to endorse Hegel's notion at a philosophical level, a large swath of the population has become convinced that so-called modern science is galloping along toward absolute knowledge. Even though we don't understand everything about the human body or brain yet today, it is clear to them that we are headed in the right direction, and that 100, 200, or possibly 500 years up the road, we will have it all figured out. In other words, a great many people have total faith today in the scientific project as what can bring us absolute knowledge; indeed, many of them *already* have complete confidence in the claims made by doctors and scientists today, despite their frequent refutation and retraction.

Lacan emphasizes, on the other hand, recent developments in science and logic that point to structural holes in knowledge, such as Gödel's incompleteness theorems (he might have mentioned the Heisenberg uncertainty principle as well, but I don't think he ever did). They point to something that cannot be known, that cannot be decisively concluded or decided upon (Gödel termed it "undecidability"), and therefore call into question the very possibility of absolute knowledge.

How is any of that relevant to psychoanalysis? Many patients, rather than asking themselves at the beginning of an analysis what they believe and what they want, ask what they *should* believe and do, as if the answers were somehow already there in religion, in psychoanalysis, or in the universe at large. A number of my analysands have commented that they felt the universe was trying to tell them something at certain times, or that they wanted to know what fate had in store for them, what the universe seemed to want from them. They were seeking an *external guarantor* of their feelings—which they took not to be things that *just are*, but rather things one *should* or *shouldn't* have—and seeking sure guidance as to how they should react to situations with their friends, partners, colleagues, and family members. The hardest thing for them to do was to say "I": I believe *x*, I want *y*, I feel *z*. They were convinced of the existence of some sort of absolute knowledge.

Some analysts are too! Freud, for example, wanted, in the case of his patient Elfriede Hirschfeld (but probably in other cases as well), to reveal to her what he believed to be the ultimate or final truth, the absolute truth about her illness, its most secret *raison d'être*, but she broke off her analysis instead (Falzeder, 1994, p. 309)![1] Lacan calls this "*la connerie de la vérité*," "the idiocy of truth." A piece of knowledge cannot be put in the place of truth, cannot serve as some sort of absolute truth—there can only be partial truths and bits of knowledge, not absolute knowledge.

Lacan was quite aware that Freud's approach to interpretation was often misguided, aiming as it did, especially early on in his work, at simply conveying a piece or chunk of supposed knowledge or truth to patients, without taking the time to bring them to formulate it themselves. And what analysands themselves formulate remains open to question and qualification indefinitely; it never becomes absolute, yet, with luck, they come to no longer care whether it is absolute or not.

On the Graph of Desire, Lacan locates all the signifiers in A. But how can we know whether we've got all of them, whether the set is complete? In fact, we can never know that, for it seems we can always add to the set. One thing we might say is that what Lacan does not locate in A is the very way in which the signifier operates by killing the thing and creating the signified: S/s, the formula for the signification process itself. Nothing in the Other can account for the signifying process itself, or "signifier-ness" (*signifiance*), and the subject must come to be in that place himself. Lacan sometimes refers to $S(\cancel{A})$ as the subject's name: not his proper name, like "Gödel," but putting his own name on his desire.

The last thing many people want to do is sign their own name to their positions and activities. They feel it is far safer to sign somebody else's name: God's name, their President's name, their commanding officer's name, their professor's name, or Pfizer's name. My priest told me that.... The scientists at Moderna say.... In this way, they keep themselves (like Sharpe's patient) on the sidelines, they have no skin in the game. If what they do turns out to be mistaken or even harmful, it wasn't their fault.

There is, in Lacan's view, something almost divine about being able to say "I"! He characterizes the Truth as saying "I speak" or "I am speaking." According to Lacan, the God of the Old Testament says about Himself,

---

[1] "She runs away from me since I could tell her the last word of the secret of her illness."

"I am what I am," or more precisely "I am what I is" (S16, p. 62), and even "I am what the I is" (p. 64).

There is something godlike in being able to say "I," and not conveying that I'm doing what I'm doing because "he said so," "she said so," or "they said I should." It is divine, Lacan seems to suggest, to be able, instead, to *speak and act in one's own name*, to *sign one's own name to things*! Hamlet is, he opines, finally able to when he utters the surprising words, "This is I, Hamlet the Dane" (V, i, 244–5).

I don't know how Shakespeare signed his name, or what texts he signed it to, but we can imagine him spelling it, at least after penning *Hamlet*, as follows: Will-I-am.

"I" has to come to take the place of (i.e., replace) the signifier of the lack in the Other:

$$\frac{\text{"I"}}{S(\cancel{A})}$$

Since there is no Other who can tell me what to do with any more justification than I can myself, I must decide for myself and go for it!

Appendix: Translator's Notes to Seminar VI

I am providing here the Translator's Note and Translator's Endnotes that I prepared to accompany the published edition of Seminar VI, *Desire and Its Interpretation* (Cambridge, UK: Polity Press, 2019), but which were not included. A few later corrections are provided here as well.

Translator's Note

Despite assistance from Héloïse Fink (with the French), Matthew Baldwin (with the Greek and Latin), and Rolf Flor (with the German), numerous errors no doubt remain here. Lacan's incredibly broad background and in-depth knowledge of numerous fields are such that I have surely misunderstood specialized terminology, overlooked references to specific authors, and just generally misinterpreted the French—Lord knows it is easy enough to do given Lacan's singular style! His oral work presents additional problems, given the number of homophonies French allows for; I have attempted to address some of these (along with alternative readings and translations, as well as likely sources of Lacan's discussions) in my endnotes. The latter are keyed to the pagination of the 2019 English edition.

© The Author(s), under exclusive license to Springer Nature Switzerland AG 2025
B. Fink, *Lacan on Desire*, The Palgrave Lacan Series,
https://doi.org/10.1007/978-3-031-76386-1

Readers who believe they have found errors of whatever kind are encouraged to send comments to me at brucefinkanalyst@gmail.com. I consider this translation to be, like my others (for which updates can be found in the form of PDFs at http://brucefink.com/bruce-fink-library/), a work in progress, and hope to improve on the text here in future editions.

Note that, although the first two chapters are quite dense, things get considerably easier as one goes along; one can even read the chapters on *Hamlet* independently of the rest and then turn to Chap. 1.

Conventions Adopted in the Text

A number of conventions were adopted in the translation. They are explained below.

Le réel is always rendered here as "the real," but it means both reality and the real (Lacan defining the latter in opposition to the imaginary and the symbolic). It is not always clear which makes the most sense at different points in Lacan's work, but given how early this seminar is, *le réel* should, I believe, be understood as "reality" in most cases here, *not* as the Lacanian real. See the following paragraphs: (45,7), (45,8), (46,1), (47,6), (65,2), (65,3), (67,3), (91,6), (92,5), (129,5), (140,1), (140,2), (323,1), (337,4), (342,7), (348,2), (349,5), (374,1), (379,5), (380,1), (381,1), (381,2), (381,3), (396,5), (397,5), (398,1), (400,4), (408,3), (417,7), (423,2), (440,2), and elsewhere.

Although *le signifiant* is generally rendered by "the signifier" here, it should kept in mind that it often refers to the signifying system as a whole or even to the signifying chain (see, for example, Chap. 8, section 2). See the following paragraphs: (35,2), (37,4), (44,2), (70,1), (78,3), (141,6), (196,6), (196,7), (324,3), (360,5), (370,5), (371,4), (409,2), and elsewhere.

Expérience analytique is always rendered here as "psychoanalytic experience," but it can often be understood as "psychoanalytic practice" (*expérience* by itself can be translated in different contexts as experience, experiment, practice, investigation, or even field). See the following paragraphs: (3,4), (4,8), (5,7), (6,1), (10,3), (10,4), (10,5), (48,3), (51,1),

(84,4), (117,4), (193,3), (193,4), (212,3), (218,4), (239,4), (240,4), (289,6), (298,9), (306,4), (358,6), (359,2), (359,6), (360,2), (360,3), (363,6), (382,1), (382,6), (392,4), (424,8), (429,3), (442,6), (471,3), (472,1), (474,5), (474,6), (475,3), (476,6), and elsewhere.

Lacan uses *articuler* and *articulation* (always translated here as "to articulate" and "articulation") constantly in this seminar, and the former can often be understood as to formulate, spell out, lay out, explain, theorize, or conceptualize, and the latter as formulation or explanation. *Articulation* also means connection or link.

Lacan also uses *au niveau de* constantly; I have usually rendered it by "at the level of," but it can also be understood less technically as "when it comes to."

En tant que (insofar as) and *pour autant que* (inasmuch as) are also used extensively, often quite vaguely; they can sometimes be rendered as "because."

The use of *génétique* (as a noun and as an adjective) is a bit atypical here, but generally refers to psychological or psychoanalytic theories of human *development*. I have resorted to circumlocutions involving the term "genesis" here, but the terms "development" and "developmental" should be kept in mind. See the following paragraphs: (76,5), (125,6), (163,7), (342,4), (348,4), and (429,6).

It finally dawned on me that "fantasmatic" is a neologism in English and that a better translation for *fantasmatique* is "fantasized" (or "fantasied").

As always, the simple word *de* poses myriad problems. Among its meanings: of, from, with, by, because of, thanks to, based on, by means of, constituted by, due to, by virtue of, since, by way of, in the form of, through, regarding, about, involved in, involving, insofar as, and as.

Lacan often uses prepositions in ways for which there are few if any precedents in French usage (e.g., *sous* in "Logical Time," *par* in "Instance of the Letter," and *de* in "Subversion of the Subject"); in this Seminar, *dans* (in) gets quite a workout and I have signaled in my notes certain places where it takes on other meanings.

All text in square brackets has been added by the translator.

Translator's Chapter by Chapter Endnotes

In these notes, the numbers in parentheses refer first to the page number of the 2019 English edition and then, after a comma, to the paragraph number (note that partial and short paragraphs are counted, as are chapter titles and the block of subheadings, counted as one paragraph, located just below each chapter title).

I   Constructing the Graph

(3,7)   Freud distinguished between what he called "psychoneuroses" (and sometimes "neuropsychoses"; SE III, pp. 45–61)—nervous disorders whose cause was psychological—and what he called "actual neuroses," nervous disorders whose cause was *not* psychological.

(3,10)   There are reasons to translate *angoisse* as "anguish" or "angst" instead of "anxiety," but I have followed Strachey's usage of "anxiety" to translate the German *Angst* in the *Standard Edition*.

(4,3)   On the "metaphor of the factory," see Seminar IV, pp. 32 and 43–4.

(4,6)   Other versions suggest that Lacan is saying: "Those who champion this new orientation very consciously borrow from Fairbairn."

(5,2)   See Freud's 1912 article "On the Universal Tendency to Debasement in the Sphere of Love" (SE XI, pp. 179–90).

(7,1)   The last sentence of this paragraph strikes me as somewhat obscure in all extant versions.

(7,2)   *L'expérience de la raison pratique* (the experience of practical reason): in this Seminar, Lacan often adds the words *l'expérience de* to surprising nouns, including desire. *Expérience* can often be translated as "practice," as in *l'expérience analytique*, "psychoanalytic practice." Here we might think of practical reason as an actual practice one engages in: "practical reason as a practice." We might, instead, translate *expérience* here as "field."

(8,1)   In English, see *A Spinoza Reader*, ed. and trans. E. Curley (Princeton: Princeton University Press, 1994), where we find: "Desire is man's very essence, insofar as it is conceived to be determined, from any given affection of it, to do something" (p. 188).

(9,5)   Instead of "We would then have the contrary:" the published edition suggests, "We would then have the contrary of what we have abandoned."

"[A]n idea of the words [*mots*] by which it would realize the desired end" should undoubtedly read "an idea of the means [*means*] by which it would realize the desired end," echoing point number (4) on page 8: "an idea of the means by which the wished-for end can be realized."

(10,4)   Other versions read *suggestive* instead of *subjective*.

(10,7)   Other versions provide *servie* instead of *asservie au langage* (subject to language), which could perhaps be understood in the figurative sense of "a psychology that is spoiled (or gets what it deserves), insofar as we can define it as the sum total of studies …"

Sensibilité might be understood here as "sensation" or "sensory perception," even though it would ordinarily be rendered as "sensibility." Lalande claims that in Kant's work *sensibilité* means *expérience*.

(11,4)   "Three is the minimum number of terms": Richards and Ogden purport to rectify Saussure's theory of the sign as encompassing the signifier and the signified, by adding a third term: the "referent."

(12,6)   "Four is the smallest possible battery": see *Écrits*, pp. 35–9.

(13,1)   *D'avant en arrière* literally means forward and back, from front to back, or from ahead to behind; less literally, it could be rendered by "one behind the other" or "back and forth."

(13,3)   Less idiomatic meanings of *tire une traite* include constituting a promissory note, discounting a draft, and drawing on the future. It could also suggest jumping to a conclusion or reckoning a sum.

(13,7)   *Seing* means mark, sign, signature, or stamp.

(14,1)   See Freud's article entitled "Negation" (SE XIX, pp. 235–9).

(14,4)   See Freud's *Beyond the Pleasure Principle* (SE XVIII, pp. 14–6).

(16,6)   "The latter [S(A)]" should perhaps be "The latter [*s*(A)]."

(17,4)   *L'expérience du désir* (The experience of desire) could instead be rendered as "The experience based on desire," "Experience involving desire," "Desire as an experience," "Experiencing desire," or even "The field of desire."

(17,6)   In English, *Hilflosigkeit* is rendered by Strachey as "helplessness"; see, for example SE XX, p. 166.

(18,4)   *Urbild*: see Lacan's paper entitled "The Mirror Stage" in *Écrits*.

(19,1)   See Lacan's paper entitled "Remarks on Daniel Lagache's Presentation: 'Psychoanalysis and Personality Structure'" in *Écrits*.

(19,4)   The French *semblable* (semblable) is often translated as "fellow man" or "counterpart," but in Lacan's usage it refers specifically to the mirroring of two imaginary others (*a* and *a'*) who *resemble* each other (or at least see themselves in each other). I have opted for the somewhat obsolete English "semblable" found, for example, in *Hamlet*: "his semblable is his mirror; and who else would trace him, his umbrage, nothing more" (V, ii, 124). It was much more recently used by Virginia Woolf in *Between the Acts* (New York: Harcourt, Brace and Company, 1941).

(19,7)   *Son niveau d'accommodation, de situation* (its proper level of correction or situation) strikes me as rather obscure; *niveau d'accommodation* is occasionally used to characterize the degree of correction of someone's vision (i.e., how strong the corrective lenses are).

(23,5)   Other versions propose that we read "the unconscious" instead of "this Other." On desire as "the metonymy of being," see, for example, *Écrits*, p. 439.

(24,1)   The French *oreille, peau* ("ear, skin") would perhaps be better heard as *oripeau*: false or deceptive shine, golden blade or knife.

II   Further Explanation

(26,5)   *Automatismes* (automatisms) are better known in English as "repetition compulsions." Here, however, the reference may be to autonomic physiological and behavioral activities.

(27,2)   Lacan's expression here, *acte de parole*, predates John Austin's and John Searle's use of the expression "speech act."

(28,6)   The Latin *subjectum* (subject) literally means that which lies under or beneath, and is thus sub-posed (supposed).

(29,4)   *Taxiématique* (taxiematic) refers to ideas that are indispensable to the construction of a discourse. At the end of the paragraph, other versions read: *c'est simplement le signe de ce que c'est la place où un autre signifiant n'est pas* (it is simply the sign of the fact that it is the place where another signifier is not).

(32,1)   "The *I* turns out to be but one object among others": see Hegel's *Phenomenology of Spirit*.

Jean-Paul Sartre, "La transcendance de l'ego," *Recherches philosophiques* VI (1936–7), pp. 85–123. In English, see *The Transcendence of the Ego: A Sketch for a Phenomenological Description* (London & New York: Routledge, 2004).

(32,2)   See Roman Jakobson's paper, "Shifters, Verbal Categories, and the Russian Verb" (1957), in Roman Jakobson, *Selected Writings*, vol. 2 (The Hague: Mouton, 1971), pp. 130–47.

(33,1)   Lacan comments on this quite extensively in Seminar III, *The Psychoses*, Chapter XXII.

(33,3)   *Soit* (so be it) and *soi* (one or oneself) are pronounced identically in certain contexts, not to mention *soie* (silk).

(33,4)   Note that Figure 1.3 looks a bit like a question mark.

(35,3)   See Freud's 1938 paper entitled "Analysis Terminable and Interminable" (SE XXIII, pp. 216–53).

(36,1)   On the "filled out" (*étoffée*) person, see Jacques Damourette and Edouard Pichon, *Des Mots à la pensée: Essai de grammaire de la langue française*, 7 vols. (Paris: Bibliothèque du français moderne, 1932–51). Note that *étoffée* (filled out) can also mean stuffed or enriched; this person is juxtaposed by Damourette and Pichon with the *subtile* (ethereal, subtle, or rarefied) person. Cf. Lacan, *Écrits*, p. 685.

(37,2)   "On this line": Lacan is undoubtedly pointing to a line on the Graph here, perhaps the upper left-to-right arrow.

(37,6)   Change "irremediable" to "irreparable."

(38,2)   The reference here is to SE IV, p. 160 n. In the fifth edition, published in 1919, Freud had already added the following passage: "The assertion that all dreams require a sexual interpretation, against which critics rage so incessantly, occurs nowhere in my *Interpretation of Dreams*" (SE V, p. 397).

(38,6)   Other versions read *à l'intérieur* (in private) instead of *à l'intérieur de soi* (in one's own mind).

(39,2)   This is the first appearance in Lacan's Seminars of the term "fundamental fantasy"; it had already been introduced in Lacan's oral delivery of "Direction of the Treatment" in July 1958.

(39,5)   "A type of little tail at the second level": this may possibly refer to the following circuit: d→($\lozenge a$)→X→($\lozenge$D).

III   The Dream about the Dead Father

(43,6)   Lacan is referring here to Serge Leclaire. The paper he gave, "*L'obsessionnel et son désir*" (The Obsessive and His Desire) was published in the journal *L'Évolution psychanalytique* 3 (1959): 383–408. Lacan made some extensive comments after Leclaire's talk.

(44,4)   "All dreams are, in a sense, dreams of convenience: they serve the purpose of prolonging sleep instead of waking up. *Dreams are the* GUARDIANS *of sleep and not its disturbers*" (SE IV, p. 233). "It is often by means of this second desire that the first is satisfied": no such claim is, to the best of my knowledge, found in Freud's work.

(44,6)   "You should understand this in the sense of 'By [coming into] being, it is satisfied'": the published version reads "*Entendez, de l'être, satisfait*," whereas other versions provide "*Entendez de l'être qui se satisfait*."

(44,7)   "Referring to being": other versions read *renvoi de l'être* instead of *renvoi à l'être*.

(45,1) Change "by being" to "by [coming into] being" in line 1, and "level of being" to "level of [coming into] being" in line 3.

(45,4) On associationism, see, for example, the work of Edward L. Thorndike, Edwin Ray Guthrie, and Clark Leonard Hull.

(47,4) See Seminar III, Chapters 17–18, and "Metaphor of the Subject" in *Écrits*.

(48,1) In this paragraph and the next, the English speaker can see an example of how the French take English words (like "flash") and change or extend their meanings.

(49,2) Other versions read "representative in the representation" instead of "representative of the representation." Strachey's translation of *Vorstellungsrepräsentanz* is "ideational representative," and his translation of *Triebregungen* is "instinctual impulses." *Unité* could, alternatively, be understood here as "unity."

(49,4) In the text we have before us, Lacan simply said that he was bracketing the subject.

(50,4) Edward Glover, "The Psycho-Analysis of Affects," *IJP* 20 (1939): 299–307.

(55,1) Cf. Freud's comment just before presenting the dream: "The strangest characteristic of unconscious (repressed) processes ... [is that] they equate reality of thought with external actuality, and wishes with their fulfillment" (SE XII, p. 225).

(55,4) Reading *croient croire* (believe we believe), as in Prévert's "*Tentative de description d'un dîner de têtes à Paris-France*" (see *Paroles* [Paris: Gallimard, 1949], p. 7), instead of *croire-croire*; Miller's note in the appendix also reads incorrectly.

(56,3) Other versions say "were different from" instead of "were nothing but."

(57,4) *Fantasme de rêve* (dream fantasy) and *fantasme(s) du rêve* appear several times in this Seminar and might also at times be rendered as "fantasy in a dream" or "fantasy that has been incorporated into a dream."

IV   Little Anna's Dream

(61,3)   The French translation Lacan is criticizing here is *La Science des rêves*, trans. I. Meyerson (Paris: Alcan, 1926).

(62,2)   "desire purportedly" should probably be "dreams purportedly" (the French transcription seems faulty here).

(62,3)   Here is Strachey's translation: "My youngest daughter, then nineteen months old, had had an attack of vomiting one morning and had consequently been kept without food all day. During the night after this day of starvation she was heard calling out excitedly in her sleep: 'Anna Fweud, stwawbewwies, wild stwawbewwies, omblet, pudden!'" (SE IV, p. 130); the dream might more accurately be rendered as "Anna Fweud, stwabewwies, wasbewwies [a child's way of pronouncing raspberries?], custad, pudden."

(62,5)   Here is Strachey's translation: "At the time she was in the habit of using her own name to express the idea of taking possession of something. The menu included pretty well everything that must have seemed to her to make up a desirable meal" (SE IV, p. 130).

(62,7)   Lacan is likely referring here to the very next dream in *The Interpretation of Dreams*: "My nephew, aged twenty-two months, had been entrusted with the duty of congratulating me on my birthday and of presenting me with a basket of cherries, which are still scarcely in season at that time of year," etc. (SE IV, pp. 130–1).

(63,1)   Here is Strachey's translation: "Pigs dream of acorns and geese dream of maize" or "What do hens dream of? - Of millet" (SE IV, p. 132 n.1).

(63,3)   The paper referred to here by Wladimir Granoff is "Ferenczi: faux problème ou vrai malentendu." It came out in *Psychanalyse: Revue de la société française de psychanalyse* 6 (1961): 255–82.

(65,3)   Reading *il les a détectés* (he detected these bits) instead of *il l'a détecté* (he detected this).

(65,4)   It might possibly make more sense to read "progressive" here instead of "regressive."

(66,3)   *Niederschriften* is usually rendered in English by notes, minutes, records, or writing down. Strachey's term for it is "registrations."

(66,4)   See *The Origins of Psychoanalysis: Letters to Wilhelm Fliess, Drafts and Notes, 1887–1902*, eds. M. Bonaparte, A. Freud, and E. Kris; trans. E. Mosbacher and J. Strachey (New York: Basic Books, 1954). Letter 52 is found on pages 173–81. *Wahrnehmung*: observing, looking after, or perceiving. Lacan decomposes the word here into *wahr* (true) and *nehmen* (to take).

(67,3)   Reading *Vor-stellungen* instead of *Vorstel-lungen*. *Vor* (pre- or before) plus *stellungen* (attitudes, positions, or stances) = *propositions* (the French here means propositions, proposals, or offers).

(67,4)   *Frayage* is Lacan's translation of Freud's *Bahnung*, which might be better rendered in English as "breach." The ball falling into the same hole seems to correspond here to Freud's "identity of perception" as opposed to "identity of thought."

(71,5)   It is not entirely clear what Lacan means by *procès* here; it could refer to progress, proceeding, procedure, temporal unfolding, or temporal process.

(73,5)   The line "*si le roi d'Angleterre était un con, tout serait permis*" (if the King of England were an idiot, all would be permitted) is found in Raymond Queneau's *On est toujours trop bon avec les femmes* (Paris: Gallimard, 1971), p. 97. Lacan discusses it in S2, pp. 127–9.

(74,7)   In certain contexts, *discours de l'Autre* can also mean "discourse about the Other."

(76,2)   Lacan may be referring here to the sort of running commentary in one's head on everything one is doing, as if one were an outside observer of oneself, that we hear about from psychotics.

V The Dream about the Dead Father

(79,3)   Freud proposes that the desire in an adult's dream is "borrowed" from the child's wishes as found in the unconscious.

(79,5)   Reading *est*, as in other versions, instead of *réside*.

(80,7)   In other versions: "they do not intentionally leave traces with the said [or what is said], but rather with traces of traces."

(81,1)   In other versions, the homonym *nom du non* (no's name or name of the no) is given.

(81,4)   See Jacques Damourette and Edouard Pichon, *Des Mots à la pensée: Essai de grammaire de la langue française* (Paris: Bibliothèque du français moderne, 1932–51), 7 vols., especially Vol. 1. Vol. 6 is useful in understanding Lacan's distinction between the subject of the statement and the subject of enunciation.

(82,1)   At least one of the exceptions here includes the use of *ne* with the verb *pouvoir*.

(83,9)   That is, the things that go through a child's mind are the very things the people around him have said.

(84,2)   The reference here is to Hegel's aesthetics ("In this very heedless boisterousness there lies the ideal feature: it is the Sunday of life which equalizes everything and removes all evil") and to Raymond Queneau's novel, *Le Dimanche de la vie*, to which this passage from Hegel's work serves as an epigraph.

(84,6)   The unnamed author of the quote is Simone Weil. See *La Pésanteur et la grâce* (1947). In English, see *Gravity and Grace* (New York: Routledge, 2002), p. 23.

(86,6)   Lacan was perhaps pointing to different points on the Graph of Desire during this passage.

(86,7)   In Strachey's rendition: "But this future, which the dream pictures as the present, has been molded by his indestructible wish into a perfect likeness of the past" (SE V, p. 621).

(88,4)   Strachey says the passage was added as a footnote in 1911 and moved into the text in 1930 (SE V, p. 430 n).

(88,7)   Other versions situate "he did not know" at the level of enunciation (on the upper line) and "he was dead" at the level of the statement.

(90,3)   *Il ne savait pas* includes an imperfect tense that can also be rendered at times as "he was not to know" (until later). The point here, however, is, I think, that the patient did not report thinking in the dream "he is dead and he does not know it" in the present tense, as might have been expected.

(92,4)   It is not clear to me whether, with *l'assumer comme celle de l'autre*, Lacan means "to take that pain upon oneself as though it were the other's" or "to view that pain as the other's." On this point, see Chapter VI, section 1, which seems to corroborate the first alternative.

(93,2)   At the beginning of Section 3, Lacan referred to the upper part of the Graph of Desire, as opposed to the lower part, as a "beyond."

(94,5)   One might change "prevalent" to "prevailing."

VI   Introducing the Object of Desire

(95,3)   Lacan seems mistaken here, the main discussion of foreclosure and discordance being found in the sixth volume of *Des mots à la pensée*.

Regarding traces, consider, for example, the fact that *pas* means footstep or track, *goutte* means drop, and *mie* originally meant crumb.

At the end of the paragraph, all extant versions read more or less as follows: "It is here that the symbolic act of foreclosure is rejected in French." The idea that foreclosure is rejected strikes me as rather odd, especially when we recall that *rejet* (rejection) was one of Lacan's early translations of Freud's *Verwerfung*, which he later rendered as *forclusion* (foreclosure). I would thus be inclined to read "*forclusion ou rejet en français*" (foreclosure or rejection in French) instead of "*forclusion est rejeté en français.*"

(96,7) Lacan refers to the article as "Analysis Finite and Infinite."

(97,3) The last five sentences are somewhat confusing in all versions of the Seminar.

(97,4) "Perpetual ignorance veiling desire": the desire in the dream would thus seem to be the desire not to know his deepest desire.

(99,6) Lacan often uses "phallus" where in English we would more commonly use "penis."

(100,4) *Artifex*, as an adjective qualifying desire here, can probably be understood as skillfully made, artistic, artificial, or ingenious. The fear here is that desire, since it is an artifice, no matter how well crafted, may not endure. See *Écrits*, p. 624.

(101,1) Jones used the Greek term "aphanisis" to refer to the "total, and of course permanent, extinction of the capacity (including opportunity) for sexual enjoyment"; see "Early Development of Female Sexuality" (1927), in *Papers on Psycho-Analysis*, 5th edition (Boston: Beacon, 1961), p. 440. According to Jones, the fear of aphanisis is more fundamental than that of castration in both sexes, castration being only a "special case" of aphanisis in boys.

(101,5) *Élan vital* is Bergson's term; see his book published in 1907, *L'Évolution créatrice* (Paris: PUF, 2006); in English, see *Creative Evolution*, trans. A. Mitchell (New York: Henry Holt and Company, 1911).

(103,4) Other versions, which are far from completely clear, suggest that it is *not* merely in our analysis that we are to try to perceive this, and that the flash is perhaps related to the "mental modes in which we are led to conceptualize it" in the "inverted Oedipus."

(105,5) All versions read "Legal phenomenology," instead of "Legal terminology"; the latter strikes me as more likely here.

(106,2) *Mammes* (breasts) does not appear to be a real word. The reference in this passage is to T. S. Eliot's poem, *The Hippopotamus*.

(106,4) See Christian Rosencreutz, *Les Noces chymiques* (Paris: Traditionnelles, 2004).

(107,1) We should read 1847 instead of 1948; see the new English translation entitled *The Misery of Philosophy: Answer to Proudhon*, trans. T. Newcomb (Cheyenne, WY: Newcomb Livraria Press, 2023). Also known as *The Poverty of Philosophy*.

(107,6) J. S. Mill, *The Subjection of Women*.

(108,1) Jones's translation of Freud's German seems rather stilted here, and Lacan's rendering of Jones's translation leaves much to be desired.

(109,5) The published version reads *Ansäße* (or *Ansässe*), and other versions read *Ansätz* or *Ansätze*, none of which seem to me to make any sense in this context. Other versions also read "immanence" instead of "imminence" in this paragraph.

(110,2) Other versions provide: $i(a)_I \diamond a(S)$.

VII Desire's Phallic Mediation

(112,1) "An imaginary frustration is [...] always related to something real": see Seminar IV.

(112,5) Reading "the pleasure principle and the reality principle" instead of "desire and the reality principle," which is found in all versions of the Seminar (presumably a slip on Lacan's part).

(113,1) Change "anything" to "any thing."

(113,6) Reading "upper line of the graph" instead of "lower line of the graph," as in all other versions and in accordance with the figure of the Graph accompanying this passage.

(115,1) Here is Trotsky's entry, dated June 26, 1935 (the French text of the Seminar erroneously says it is on the last page of the diary):

> Last night, or rather early this morning, I dreamed I had a conversation with Lenin. Judging by the surroundings, it was on a ship, on the third-class deck. Lenin was lying in a bunk; I was either standing or sitting near him, I am not sure which. He was questioning me anxiously about my illness. "You seem to have accumulated nervous fatigue, you must rest..." I answered that I had always recovered from fatigue quickly, thanks to my native *Schwungkraft*, but that this time the trouble seemed to lie in some

deeper processes ... "Then you should *seriously* (he emphasized the word) consult the doctors (several names) ...." I answered that I already had many consultations and began to tell him about my trip to Berlin; but looking at Lenin I recalled that he was dead. I immediately tried to drive away this thought, so as to finish the conversation. When I had finished telling him about my therapeutic trip to Berlin in 1926, I wanted to add, "This was after your death"; but I checked myself and said, "After you fell ill...." [pp. 145–6]

(115,4) I have followed the stenography in the second sentence of this paragraph, instead of the published version, which strikes me as somewhat obscure.

(116,2) Other versions suggest, "the desire that he had long dominated that had now subdued him."

(116,7) Reading a–a' instead of a'–a.

(117,1) The prime on a' in the upper righthand corner of the L Schema is missing.

(117,2) "Oblativity" is a supposed tendency to give to others selflessly or disinterestedly that was discussed in French analytic texts of the 1950s (the adjectival form is "oblative"). The term was introduced by Laforgue in 1926 and was rendered as "self-sacrifice" in Lacan's "Some Reflections on the Ego," *IJP* 34, *1* (1953): 17. It is often a synonym for altruism.

(119,2) "The requirement that the subject manifest himself – beyond all of that – in his being" – that is, as a being of desire, as a being who desires.

(120,2) The *objet achevé* (fully developed object) may be a reference to Erikson's 1956 notion of the "total object" and "total object relations." See E. H. Erikson, "The problem of ego identity," *JAPA* 4 (1956): 56–121. "Male and female created He them" is found in Jones's paper, "The Phallic Phase," in *Papers on Psychoanalysis*, 5th edition (Boston: Beacon, 1961), p. 484.

(121,2) The French text, based on highly inaccurate stenography, is quite faulty here.

(122,1)   Reading *Schlagephantasie*, as in Freud's German text, instead of *Schlagfantasie*.

(122,2)   On hatred as targeting being, see the end of Seminar XX on concierges and rats.

(122,5)   Lacan renders this instead as, "The fantasy is accompanied by a high degree of pleasure, and is carried out in an altogether significant way."

(123,4)   Certain versions add a comma, reading, *un être, sujet à vouloir* (a being who has a will), instead of *comme un être sujet à vouloir* (a being who is subject to will).

(123,7)   Picasso, *Le Désir attrapé par la queue* (Paris: Gallimard, 1995). In English, *Desire Caught by the Tail* (New York: Citadel, 1962).

(125,2)   Lacan is presumably referring here to the following sentence in Addendum B to *Inhibitions, Symptoms, and Anxiety*: "*Es ist nun ein wichtiger Fortschritt in unserer Selbstbewahrung, wenn eine solche traumatische Situation von Hilflosigkeit nicht abgewartet, sondern vorhergesehen, erwartet wird,*" which is translated by Strachey as follows: "The individual will have made an important advance in his capacity for self-preservation if he can foresee and expect a traumatic situation of this kind which entails helplessness, instead of simply waiting for it to happen" (SE XX, p. 166). Note that *abgewartet* is a conjugation of *abwarten*.

(126,3)   The published version reads "Today, we have identified the phallus with *a*." Other versions are vaguer, suggesting that the reference is more immediate, hence to the subject or to "the other that the subject bears within himself."

(126,6)   See S1, p. 78, and *Écrits*, p. 564. "Spherical rays": Lacan presumably means rays produced by a spherical mirror.

(128,5)   The end of this paragraph might perhaps be understood as "a point where what you might grasp as extrapolations of the erotic blueprint [*épure*] between subjects is eliminated." It is not clear to me what *point de réduction* (point of reduction) means. "Vanishing point"?

VIII The Little Cough as a Message

(136,1) "That is itself marked by enunciation" (*indice d'énonciation*) could instead be rendered by "that has an enunciation index, rating, or factor."

(136,5) We find the following formula in the stenography: $E(e^E)$. It might well read, instead (and following Lacan's later use of *indice*), $E(e_E)$.

(137,3) I have followed other versions in which the last sentence of this paragraph is phrased as though it were a comment the dreamer makes about a dream.

(141,4) "The bridge formed by the ships on the Bosphorus": see Herodotus's *Histories*, Book 4.

(142,1) Ella Sharpe, *Dream Analysis* (London: The Hogarth Press and the Institute of Psycho-Analysis, 1937), Chapter V, "Analysis of a Single Dream."

(145,3) I cannot locate anything the patient says in the text that goes in the direction indicated in the first sentence of this paragraph. This is thus an extrapolation on Lacan's part, as we see in the next class, and the stenography is presumably somewhat faulty here.

(146,5) Here is the first part of the paragraph:

> On the day when the patient related to me the dream I have selected for this chapter I did not hear him coming upstairs. I never do. There is a carpet on the stairs, but that is not the reason. One patient comes up two stairs at a time and I hear just the extra thud; another hurries and I detect the hustle; another is sure to knock a suitcase or umbrella or fist on the banisters. (p. 129)

(148,2) Sharpe was a co-head teacher at the Hucknall Pupil Teachers Training College. Sharpe writes, "To draw this patient's attention to a manifestation of the unconscious is to stop it" (p. 130).

(150,4) Reading "οὖτις," as in Homer's text, instead of "*où est-il?*" The correct term is provided in Chapter XII of this Seminar.

IX   The Fantasy about the Barking Dog

(152,3)   In context, Sharpe seems to mean just one dream as opposed to several: Chapter V of her book is entitled "Analysis of a Single Dream" (p. 125).

(154,3)   According to Sharpe, he "got hold of his tormentor round the neck and held him playfully in a strangle grip and warned him never to tease him again" (p. 147).

(159,2)   The French here is quite ambiguous and could, alternatively, be rendered as "the signifier for the Other" or "the signifier that concerns the Other."

(161,1)   We should probably read "question" or "interrogation" here instead of "interpretation" (a likely slip on Lacan's part, as he is referring to Sharpe's question to her patient: "And why cough before coming in here?").

(161,2)   For Lacan's comments on "scent," see *Écrits*, pp. 221, 280, 389, 407 n. 20, and 509, and S4, p. 79. Lebovici mentions that her patient at one point believed he detected the smell of urine in her office.

(161,7)   Other versions read *l'autre phase* (the other phase) instead of *l'autre face* (the flip side).

(162,3)   Other versions read *moi* (ego or me) instead of *moyen* (means).

(163,4)   Lacan may be referring here to his paper "In Memory of Ernest Jones: On His Theory of Symbolism," which he sketched out from January to March, 1959 (see, in particular, *Écrits*, p. 593). He may, alternatively, although this seems less likely given the way he refers to his paper in this class, be referring to comments he made after Chaim Perelman's talk at the Société française de philosophie, comments that were later written up as "Metaphor of the Subject" (see, in particular, *Écrits*, p. 757). See, also, *Écrits*, p. 682.

(163,6)   The first sentence of this paragraph does not seem to be included in other versions.

(163,7)   We might consider reading "reactions" instead of "reflections" in the last line of this paragraph.

(163,8) "How does the signifier enter into their world?": other versions read, instead, "How do children enter into the world of language?"

(166,4) See *Écrits*, p. 593, where we see that Lacan borrows this example from Ernest Jones.

(166,6) "Marked and shot through and through with the signifying element": other versions read, *marqué par le travers de l'élément signifiant*, which strikes me as unclear.

(167,11) Lacan translates this as "memory of a dog masturbating," which is practical (albeit inaccurate) as the English construction is quite difficult to render in French.

(167,12) Reading *scène* (scene) instead of *schéma* (schema).

(169,3) Reading *un signifiant* (a signifier) instead of *signifiant* (signifying).

(170,3) Lacan is mistaken here: the patient suddenly *thought* of the dream (see quote on S6, p. 143), which doesn't imply he suddenly *remembered* it.

X   The Image of the Inside-Out Glove

(173,1) "The call loops back on itself in order to instate itself in what I have sometimes called 'full speech'": other versions suggest that "the Other's discourse loops back on itself, and the call on the Other for the satisfaction of a need is instated [or: established] in relation to the Other in what I have sometimes called 'full speech.'"

(173,2) *De moi comme moi* could, alternatively, be rendered as "of myself as an ego." Other versions read: "the simple fact that someone speaks of me as me…."

(173,3) The last sentence of the paragraph refers to the homology between desire and the ego mentioned three paragraphs back; compare their positions in the upper and lower parts of the Graph of Desire.

(178,2) "China" likely comes into the limerick because of the paucity of words in English that truly rhyme with "vagina."

(178,3) Lacan perhaps found this limerick in the following collection: *The Limerick: A Facet of Our Culture*. Privately printed in Mexico City in 1944.

(179,5) "Underscores that it is difficult not to consider": other versions do not include the word "not" here.

(182,4) Here are the lyrics to the song, "Where Did You Get That Hat?"

> Now how I came to get this hat is very strange and funny
> Grandfather died and left to me his property and money
> And when the Will it was read out they told me straight and flat
> If I would have his money I must always wear his hat.
>
> *Chorus*: 'Where did you get that hat? Where did you get that tile?
> Isn't it a nobby one and just the proper style.
> I should like to have one just the same as that.
> Wherever I go they shout "Hello, where did you get that hat?"
>
> If I go to the Opera house in the opera season
> There's someone sure to shout at me without the slightest reason
> If I go to a Concert Hall to have a jolly spree
> There's someone in the party who is sure to shout at me.
>
> Chorus:
>
> At twenty-one I thought I would to my sweetheart get married
> The people in the neighbourhood had said too long we'd tarried
> So off to church we went right quick determined to get wed
> I had not long been in there when the parson to me said,
>
> Chorus:
>
> I once tried hard to be MP but failed to get elected
> Upon a tub I stood round which a thousand folks collected
> And I had dodged the eggs and bricks (which was no easy task)
> When one man cried, "A question I the candidate would ask"
>
> SPOKEN: I told him I was ready to reply to any question that could be put to me. The man said, "Thousands of British working people are anxiously awaiting enlightenment on the subject on which I am about to address you. It is a question of national importance, in fact, THE great problem of the day, and that is, sir...."

Chorus:

When Colonel South, the millionaire, gave his last garden party
I was amongst the guests who had a welcome true and hearty
The Prince of Wales was also there and my heart jumped with glee
When I was told the Prince of Wales would like a word with me.

Chorus:

(185,4)   I have been unable to find the expression *subir une couverture* anywhere. It could possibly relate to his being pinned into his sheets or strapped into his pram as a child (p. 136), or being overshadowed or covered by the overhanging tip of the cave.

(188,7)   In Latin, *vagina* means sheath or scabbard for a sword.

(189,3)   Lacan seems to confuse "he attended a function" (p. 143) with the idea that he went to a certain place for "professional reasons."

(189,5)   As a certain amount of text is obviously missing in this paragraph, I have followed the stenography.

(189,6)   "in English society" should be changed to "in the English psychoanalytic society."

Klein's "combined parent-figure" (also referred to as the "combined parent") denotes an infantile fantasy in which the parents are united in a permanent sexual act, the mother containing the father's penis or the whole father, the father containing the mother's breast or the whole mother. Klein developed the concept in her book *The Psycho-Analysis of Children* (London: Hogarth Press, 1932), pp. 103–4.

XI   Sacrificing the Taboo Queen

(191,8)   The French here condenses two different quotes from Sharpe's text.

(192,5)   Note that Lacan often uses the word "phallus" when Sharpe simply says "penis."

(193,1)   Sharpe tells us she is "justified [in doing so] by virtue of past analyses" [p. 143], a move Lacan himself makes in the next chapter.

(195,2) I have simplified the French to keep the associations in the order in which we find them in Sharpe's text.

(195,3) It is unclear to me what passage in Sharpe's text could possibly have given Lacan the sense that the man was thought to be that extraordinary, much less a conman, by the patient.

(196,7) See the discussion of the game of chess and of the sacrifice of one's queen in chess at the end of this chapter.

(197,1) Reading *d'entrainement d'angoisse* (provoking of anxiety) instead of *d'entrainement, d'angoisse*.

(200,4) "*Common Book of Prayer*": this inversion, found in the stenography as well, was perhaps a slip on Lacan's part or perhaps intentional.

(204,6) *Dame* (queen) also means lady.

(206,5) "Poorly translated it": Lacan had presumably mistranslated this line in a prior class.

(206,7) Other versions read *serrer son jeu* (play tougher) instead of *serrer son cul* (clench his sphincter); the word is missing in the stenography.

(207,3) Although ostensibly quoting Sharpe, the French curiously goes further than "he liked it" here, reading "I love it" in English.

(207,4) *Non-motivé*: less literally put, desire is what has no rhyme or reason.

(209,2) From Carroll's poem, *The Mad Gardener's Song*.

XII The Laughter of the Immortal Gods

(211,2) By giving *en finir avec* as a translation for "to get," Lacan is presumably thinking of an expression like "to get someone" or "you're going to get it."

(211,5) Lacan may well be saying that we should limit the extension or importance we give to a specific signifier here–"hood" or "vagina"–not to the signifying order in general. Other versions read *caractère du signifiant* instead of *registre du signifiant*, implying perhaps that the *image* of the hood is not that important as a signifier here, whereas to Sharpe it is essential.

(214,4) *Assumer* corresponds to the English "to assume" in the sense of to take on (as in "to assume a responsibility"), but also implies taking in, adopting, incorporating, owning, dealing with, and coming to terms with. In contexts like this, I often translate *assumer* as "to assume" and *assomption* as "assumption."

(214,5) This might be connected with Freud's notion that during the castration complex, a boy is faced with losing his penis if he refuses to give up his mother as his primary love object. He is led to weigh the two against each other and choose.

(215,2) "She *is* without having it": another version reads: "she is it without having it," which we find again on p. 234, paragraph 4.

(216,6) See "The Mirror Stage" in *Écrits* and "Family Complexes" in *Autres Écrits*.

(218,2) *The Confessions of St. Augustine*, trans. J. G. Pilkington (New York: The Heritage Press, 1963), p. 7. The rendition in the Seminar is not identical to the one found in *Écrits*, p. 114, where, among other things, *amer* (bitter) is replaced by *empoisonné* (envenomed).

(220,1) That is, according to Klein, the phallus (or penis) takes the place of the breast.

(221,6) The French should probably read *j'aime bien ça*, but Lacan perhaps wanted to exaggerate what the patient actually said, which was reported by Sharpe as "he liked it" (p. 146).

(223,1) "He has no memories of his life prior to age 11": the patient says his friend "who can do impersonations" remembers *her* childhood well (p. 134).

(223,2) He presumably "caught up with his sister" when he turned 11, and "encountered her at the very point at which" they had lost their father. Is Lacan suggesting that the boy had abandoned his sister in the interim?

(224,3) The French erroneously reads: "the piquant fantasy he says he had again not long ago," whereas the case study tells us nothing about when he had the fantasy (p. 132).

(224,5) "Further disintegrated" compared, perhaps, to when his sister served as *i(a)* for him.

(225,3) The usual expression is *entre l'arbre et l'écorce il ne faut pas mettre son doigt*. Here it is inverted.

(228,6) *Le furet* (slippery, darting animal) is a reference to a game in which a group of people sit in a circle and quickly pass a small object – referred to as *le furet*, though a *furet* is literally a ferret – from hand to hand, while a player standing in the middle of the circle tries to guess which hand holds the *furet*.

(229,2) The reference here should instead be to Ovid's *Metamorphosis*, Book IV, v. 167–89.

(229,4) *Aphanisos* might be construed to be a substantive use of an adjective formed from the verb *aphanizein*, "to make disappear." *Aphanisos* as an adjective would mean "making disappear" and as a nominal substantive, "one who makes disappear."

(229,5) The Greek is found in Strabo's *Geography* (2.3.6), where Strabo refers to Aristotle's discussion of Homer's *Iliad*. Strabo mentions a traveler, Eudoxus of Cyzicus, who, according to Posidonius, allegedly sailed around the horn of Africa (Geog. 2.3.4). Strabo regards Posidonius's story as false and likens Posidonius to Plato, who quoted Solon as evidence of the credibility of the story of the disappearance of Atlantis. Strabo suggests that Posidonius should rather have said "he who brought it into existence can also cause it to disappear, as the poet did the wall of the Achivi," which is a reference to Homer's *Iliad*, vii. 436, where a wall is described which, like Atlantis, Strabo and his contemporaries believe never existed in the first place.

XIII Impossible Action

(234,4) To "be it without having it" is actually a slightly different formulation from the ones he had provided in earlier classes; the same is true of "being and not being the phallus."

(234,7) The French curiously reads "in 1910–1914" instead of just "1914."

(241,2) Lacan is presumably thinking here of Nietzsche's *Birth of Tragedy*.

(241,5) "The Death of Hamlet's Father" is the last paper in Ernest Jones, *Essays in Applied Psychoanalysis*, vol. 1 (London: Hogarth, 1951). I have tried to correct things in this paragraph and the next, as the French erroneously reads: "It is the father himself who informs us of it, as Horatio regrets, telling Hamlet, 'There needs no ghost, my lord, come from the grave, to tell us this.'"

(242,1) Lacan refers here to Claudius's crime as Oedipal, even though Claudius was the king's brother, not his son.

(242,3) *Articulation* (articulation) can also be understood as connection or link.

(244,7) Ophelia's suicide is considered ambiguous in the play, yet when it is first mentioned, it is said that a branch she was standing on broke:

> There, on the pendent boughs her coronet weeds
> Clambering to hang, an envious sliver broke;
> When down her weedy trophies and herself
> Fell in the weeping brook. (IV, vii, 170–3)

(245,7) At the end of this sentence, one might prefer to read *au sens où il est dans le psychisme du créateur* ("in the sense that it is in the psyche of the creator," presumably Shakespeare), as in other versions, instead of *au sens où il est, dans le psychisme, créateur*.

(246,7) "Mortal coil" is a poetic term that means the burden or troubles of everyday life and the strife and suffering of the world, "coil" referring to the fuss, bustle, or ado of daily living.

XIV The Desire Trap

(250,1) According to the authors of *The Complete Pelican Shakespeare*, which I have relied on here:

> *Hamlet* is preserved in three distinct but related early texts: first, the corrupt and abbreviated acting version in the "bad" quarto of 1603; second, the version "newly imprinted and enlarged to almost as much again as it was, according to the true and perfect coppie"

in the "good" quarto of 1604–5 (now usually regarded, but without complete assurance, as printed from Shakespeare's own draft); and third, the version in the 1623 folio (now usually regarded, but again without complete assurance, as printed from the prompt-book of Shakespeare's acting company or from the good quarto altered after reference to such a prompt-book). (p. 932)

(251,4)   "Cyclothymic": today we might say "manic-depressive" or "bipolar."

(254,2)   See Richard Loening, *Die Hamlet-Tragödie Shakespeares* (Stuttgart: Verlag J. G. Cotta'schen Buchhandlung, 1893).

(255,3)   The five lectures that Freud gave in German at Clark University were published in English translation as "The Origin and Development of Psychoanalysis" in the *American Journal of Psychology* 21, no. 2 (1910): 181–218. Jones's paper, "Freud's Theory of Dreams," came out in the same issue of the same journal (pp. 283–308).

(257,8)   *Trop vous faire tarder* (draw this out interminably) could instead be rendered as "keep you too long today."

(258,4)   An officer, Bernardo, was actually saying that "The bell [was] then beating one" when the ghost appeared the night before the night the play begins (I, i, 39).

(258,9)   Actually, Ophelia tells us that it was "twice two months," thus four months (III, ii, 123).

(259,4)   It is not entirely clear what part of the ghost's speech Lacan is referring to here, but he might be rather freely interpreting the following lines:

Taint not thy mind, nor let thy soul contrive
Against thy mother aught. Leave her to heaven
And to those thorns that in her bosom lodge
To prick and sting her. (I, v, 85–8)

(259,5)   Yet the ghost, after telling Hamlet he was killed by Claudius, clearly says:

> If thou hast nature in thee, bear it not.
> Let not the royal bed of Denmark be
> A couch for luxury and damned incest. (I, v, 81–3)

(262,8)   The King actually cries, "Give me some light. Away!" and Polonius cries "Lights, lights, lights!" (III, ii, 259–60).

(263,3)   "The disguised dimension of truth that I somewhere called its 'fictional structure'": see *Écrits*, 2006, pp. 375–6.

(264,3)   It is actually the ghost who tells Hamlet that the father died "in the blossoms of [his] sin" (I, v, 76).

(265,7)   "Conceit," in Shakespeare's usage, probably does not mean what Lacan thinks it means, and can be quite equivocal, meaning fancy, opinion, imagination, wit, trinket, ingenuity, brooding, and so on.

(267,5)   What is he whose grief
> Bears such an emphasis? whose phrase of sorrow
> Conjures the wand'ring stars, and makes them stand
> Like wonder-wounded hearers? This is I,
> Hamlet the Dane. [V, i, 241–5]

XV   The Mother's Desire

(269,6)   John Dover Wilson, *What Happens in* Hamlet (Cambridge: Cambridge University Press, 1935).

(270,1)   Other versions add at the end of this paragraph: "Jones makes very apt remarks that I find myself occasionally repeating."

(272,5)   "In a different text": see "A Psychoanalytic Study of Hamlet" in *Essays in Applied Psychoanalysis* (London: The International Psychoanalytical Press, 1923), p. 27.

(276,4)   *Le discours de l'Autre* can at times be translated as "(the) discourse about the Other," but not, I think, in the present case.

(278,2)   Ernest Jones, "A Psychoanalytic Study of Hamlet" in *Essays in Applied Psychoanalysis* (London: The International Psychoanalytical Press, 1923), p. 29.

(278,4)   *Beatus possidens* can be rendered as lucky (or happy) possessor, or owner by default. *Sensible*: the French here is ambiguous; Lacan may have been using "sensible" in its English sense; the editor has added the words "in the play" after it. The text could thus read instead: "this rationale is nevertheless more sensible*."

(279,2)   Ernest Jones, "A Psychoanalytic Study of Hamlet" in *Essays in Applied Psychoanalysis* (London: The International Psychoanalytical Press, 1923), p. 35.

(281,3)   Lacan seems to confuse here the number of years the first gravedigger (or clown) has been a sexton, thirty years, with the number of years since Yorick died, twenty-three (V, i); Hamlet says he himself kissed Yorick's lips "I know not how oft."

(281,6)   *L'appétit vient en mangeant* is a common French expression, and the translation "appetite comes with eating" is from a mid-seventeenth-century translation of Rabelais's *Gargantua* into English. Cf. Hamlet's comment in Act I, Scene 2: "As if increase of appetite had grown / By what it fed on."

(286,1)   Other versions more plausibly suggest that the unconscious circuit begins, not at Δ at the bottom right, but at the extreme left of the top left-to-right vector.

(286,7)   *La Psychanalyse d'aujourd'hui* ["Contemporary Psychoanalysis"] (Paris: PUF, 1956).

XVI   There is No Other of the Other

(292,2)   "The ghost that the sentinels have already seen twice": reading "twice" instead of "once" in accordance with Act I, Scene 1. *En-bas*: Perhaps a reference to Victor Hugo's translation of the end of Act III, Scene 3.

(292,3)   *Coleridge's Lectures on Shakespeare and Other Poets and Dramatists* (New York: E. P. Dutton and Co., 1907), p. 141.

(292,4)   Actually, the clock struck one the "last night of all," i.e., the second time the sentinels saw the ghost.

(292,5)   In class, Lacan rendered this line in French as "*Qu'est-ce que c'est de tuer un homme, le temps de dire 'un,'*" "What is it to kill a man, the time it takes to say 'one.'"

(292,6)   In Shakespeare's usage, "truant" can also mean unfaithful, absentee, remiss, rogue, knave, rascal, and so on.

(295,3)   Reading *nous regardons Hamlet* (when we look at Hamlet) rather than *nous nous regardons Hamlet.* The stenography reads: *nous nous regardons dans Hamlet,* we look at ourselves in Hamlet.

(296,3)   See, in this context, Figure 7.1, not Figure 5.1.

(297,1)   The question here would seem to be "Who killed the father?"

(297,7)   Line 4 should read $s(A)$, not $s(\cancel{A})$.

(298,2)   "*Flectere si nequeo superos, Acheronta movebo,*" from Virgil's *Aeneid,* is translated in *The Interpretation of Dreams,* as "If I cannot bend the Higher Powers, I will move the Infernal regions."

(299,1)   "Fecund delusion": a likely reference to Lacan's *Family Complexes,* Chap. 2, Part 1, where we find the phrase: "*phase féconde du délire,*" the fruitful or fecund phase of the delusion.

(299,2)   *Répondre de* can also take on the senses of "explain," "define," "account for," "protect," "deal with," "take care of," and "take responsibility for." "Truth without truth": one might instead read, "truth without Truth."

(300,2)   *Poussée vitale* is mentioned in a similar context in Seminar V. The term resembles Bergson's *élan vital,* "vital impulse," mentioned in Chap. 6 above. *Poussée* is the usual French translation of Freud's *Drang,* one of the components of the drive, often rendered in English as "pressure"; see SE XIV, p. 122. The last sentence of this paragraph is found only in the published edition.

(302,5)   Lacan's French rendition here differs quite significantly from all the versions of the English text I consulted (II, iv).

(304,2) See Emile Boisacq, *Dictionnaire étymologique de la langue grecque, étudiée dans ses rapports avec les autres langues indo-européennes* (Heidelberg and Paris: C. Winter, 1907–14).

(305,3) In the third class of the Seminar, Lacan quoted Simone Weil as saying, "To ascertain exactly what the miser whose treasure was stolen lost: thus we should learn much."

XVII   Ophelia, the Object

(308,1) *Le sujet primordial de la demande* (the primordial subject to whom demands are addressed, but literally: the primordial subject of demand) can refer to the primordially demanding subject, namely, the parent or child who makes demands, or to the primordial subject to whom demands are addressed. Lacan seems, in this context, to be intending the parental subject, presumed to be omnipotent, to whom the child's demands are addressed. In talking, a few pages further on, about ($\not{S}\lozenge D$), he seems to be emphasizing the subject faced with the Other's demands (e.g., demands that the child eat, become toilet trained, etc.).

(310,4) Lacan is probably referring to "the volume" entitled *La Psychanalyse d'aujourd'hui*, mentioned in earlier classes of this Seminar.

(313,5) If it had not been clear to certain readers of this Seminar that object *a* here is imaginary, not real – that is, not the real cause of desire that it becomes in Lacan's later work – the equation of *a* with the "imaginary other" in the last sentence of this paragraph should clarify things.

(313,6) Lacan's commentary on Genet's *The Balcony* can be found in *Le Séminaire de Jacques Lacan, Livre V, Les formations de l'inconscient* (Paris: Seuil, 1998), pp. 263–8. In English, see *The Seminar of Jacques Lacan, Book V: Formations of the Unconscious*, trans. R. Grigg (Cambridge: Polity, 2017).

(318,1) The text in brackets here is found only in other versions.

(318,2) Pascal said, "*Les hommes sont si nécessairement fous que ce serait être fou par un autre tour de folie de n'être pas fou*" (*Pensées*, number 412/414), which can be translated as "Men are so necessarily crazy that it would be crazy, by another twist of madness, not to be crazy," "Men are so necessarily mad that not to be mad would amount to another form of madness," or "Men are so inevitably mad that not to be mad would be to give a mad twist to madness."

(318,7) In the previous class, we find *ophallos*, not *omphalos*; the latter means navel or hub, and was a symbol for the center of the world. See Ella F. Sharpe, "An Unfinished Paper on *Hamlet*: Introduction and Extracts" in *Collected Papers on Psycho-analysis* (London: Hogarth, 1950).

(319,4) Polonius asks this as a question in the spot in the above quote where [...] appears. *Estrangement* is rarely used in contemporary French; the *Trésor de la langue françoise* by Jean Nicot, dating back to 1606, defines the verb *estranger* as "*séparer et mettre hors de soy quelque chose, et la réduire en respect et condition de chose étrange*" (to separate and distance something from oneself, turning it into something foreign). *Estrangement* as a noun formerly meant the result of such distancing or alienating of oneself and of what is familiar. It is not clear if Lacan intended the old French or the contemporary English term here.

(321,5) "Turgidity" would probably be better here than "turgescence."

(321,7) "[L]ong purples, / That liberal shepherds give a grosser name" (IV, vii, 168–9).

XVIII Mourning and Desire

(328,3) In hunting, *hallali* implies the final moment of the hunt when the animal being pursued is exhausted and the hunters and dogs go in for the kill.

(329,5) "Fight to the death of pure prestige": see Hegel's *Phenomenology of Spirit*, trans. A. V. Miller (Oxford: Oxford University Press, 1977), section B, IV; the precise wording here seems to come from Alexandre Kojève's *Introduction to the Reading of Hegel:*

Lectures on the Phenomenology of Spirit (Ithaca, NY: Cornell University Press, 1980); see, for example, p. 7.

(330,3)   It is not clear to me that Lacan has correctly grasped the import of Hamlet's lines here (V, ii, 117-19), which suggest that Laertes has no equal or semblable: only his mirror image is worthy of him; he is head and shoulders above everyone else. Anyone who would try to be like him can be but a poor imitation or approximation ("his umbrage"). Hamlet is thus *not* implying that he and Laertes are semblables. (He may simultaneously be mocking Osric's overblown, precious courtier's speech.)

(330,4)   "He who is my ideal ego": the stenography suggests that Lacan made a slip of the tongue here and said "ego-ideal" instead of the quite obviously intended "ideal ego."

(332,3)   Lacan may have been unaware of other meanings of "foil" in Shakespeare's usage, as in check, repulse, setback, defeat, flaw, blemish, disgrace, overthrow, or undoing, suggesting that Hamlet will *foil* Laertes' designs.

(333,8)   See Daniel Lagache, "Deuil pathologique" in *La Psychanalyse* 2 (1956): 45–74.

(334,5)   Dan Collins (2022) comments on the import of Hamlet's lines here (V, i, 275-9) as follows:

> Hamlet is speaking in some heat and anger. The sense seems to be, "Even if my opponent were Hercules, it doesn't matter: cats will be cats. But look out (cat) because dogs will always eventually come out on top." The saying "Every dog will have his day" was already proverbial according to the sources. What Hamlet adds is the implication that Laertes is a "cat." So, Laertes may have been acting in a Herculean manner (raging), but Hamlet doesn't take him seriously. A triple insult: "1) You're raging like a lunatic, but 2) I take it no more seriously than a pussy cat's meows, still, 3) if you're a cat, then I'm a dog—and you'll get yours." ("Mew" also has a verbal meaning: to confine, to enclose, to coop up. Hamlet may thus also be suggesting, "A cat may trap or box in the dog, but the dog will eventually get out.")

What's remarkable about this speech is that Hamlet seems genuinely shocked that Laertes is raging and angry at him: "What is the reason that you use me thus? / I loved you ever." Hamlet seems to completely disregard the fact that he killed Laertes's father (he seems to disregard, then, that Laertes's cause is the mirror of his own).

Afterwards, though, Hamlet seems to realize that Laertes is his counterpart and appears to regret the entire encounter:

> But I am very sorry, good Horatio,
> That to Laertes I forgot myself;
> For by the image of my cause I see
> The portraiture of his.

In other words, he's no longer seeing them as cat and dog. He's also implying that to "forget himself" is to forget, or to neglect in the heat of passion, one of his primary identifications, to Laertes, the son of a murdered father. He still doesn't quite get that the two cases are not equal because Hamlet himself is the one who murdered Laertes's father. Even this failure to realize this point, though, is telling: Hamlet is in the Claudius position here.

(336,4) "Out of his mind": the grammar of other versions might suggest a different rendering of *hors de lui*, such that Laertes embraces the object that is "outside of himself."

(337,3) See *Confucius, Li chi: Book of Rites. An Encyclopedia of Ancient Ceremonial Usages, Religious Creeds, and Social Institutions*, trans. J. Legge (New Hyde Park, NY: University Books, 1967).

XIX Phallophanies

(339,1) On "phallophanies" (appearances or manifestations of the phallus) see the very end of this chapter. See, also, Lacan's comment in Seminar VIII: "What we call aggressiveness always presents itself in obsessive neurosis as aggression toward the form of the Other's appearance that, on another occasion, I called 'phallophany,' the Other insofar as he can present himself as the phallus" (p. 246).

(339,7) Reading *restes* (leftovers) instead of *reliefs* (contours, projections).

(340,1) Reading "last time" instead of "the time before last." On the dream's navel, see *The Interpretation of Dreams*, SE V, p. 525. Note that in the prior class, Lacan had said that the death of a loved one "constitutes a *Verwerfung*, a hole, [not in the symbolic] but in reality."

(342,3) Regarding "Life is a dream," see Jacques Vallée des Barreaux's poem, *La vie est un songe*.

(344,4) On the "beautiful soul," see Hegel's *Phenomenology of Spirit*, trans. A. V. Miller (Oxford: Oxford University Press, 1977), p. 383.

(344,5) Lacan's translation of Hamlet's lines includes "*que je ne sois né jamais*" (would that I had never been born), which evokes Oedipus's line from *Oedipus at Colonus* "not to be born" (line 1224).

(345,4) Lacan very often uses the word "phallus" where Freud uses the word "penis."

(345,7) Reading "gratification" instead of "the phallus," as in the stenography. "Lassitude" here perhaps refers to Freud's term *hoffnungslosen* in the first paragraph of the paper, translated by Strachey as "hopeless longing" (SE XIX, p. 173); this hopeless longing is not, however, for the penis/phallus, but for the love and affection of the beloved parent.

(347,4) The stenography would have us read something quite different starting with the second sentence of this paragraph: "'Narcissistic' here explains the following to us: it is precisely in mourning, insofar as nothing is satisfied by mourning – and nothing here can satisfy, since the loss of the phallus experienced as such is the very outcome of the gamut run of his whole relationship with what occurs in the locus of the Other, that is, in the field organized by the symbolic in which his demand for love has begun to express itself. He is at the end and his loss in this case is a radical one."

(349,1)   Other versions provide a far more complete table after the one given in the text, to which I have added a few notations that grow out of Lacan's commentary here:

Agent	Lack	Object
Real father	Castration	imaginary phallus
$\emptyset$	symbolic debt	i
R	S	
Symbolic mother	Frustration	real breast
A	imaginary displeasure	r
S	I	
Imaginary father	Deprivation	symbolic phallus
$(-\varphi)$ [?]	real hole	s
I	R	

(350,3)   Lacan seems to be referring here to variations on the formula for fantasy, as discussed in *Écrits*, pp. 823–6.

(351,3)   We should perhaps read "appearance" instead of "disappearance" here, although the latter may refer to the subject as "a negative object" $(-\varphi)$.

(351,7)   "A man" like any other may be a reference to Hamlet's comment to Horatio about his father:

> He was a man, take him for all in all,
> I shall not look upon his like again. [Act I, Scene 2]

In which case the text should probably read, "'a man' unlike any other," but it appears that Lacan misunderstood the meaning of the English here, given the sentence that follows.

Lacan might instead be referring to Hamlet's comment to his mother:

> A combination and a form indeed,
> Where every god did seem to set his seal,
> To give the world assurance of a man:
> This was your husband … [III, iv, 61–4]

(352,4)   *Génie étonné* (daunted genius) is from Racine's *Britannicus*: "*mon génie étonné tremble devant le sien*," which has been rendered by George Dillon as "my daunted genius trembles before hers" (v. 506).

(352,6)   See the final pages of Chapter VIII in Freud's *Group Psychology and the Analysis of the Ego*.

(354,2)   Reading "nought" instead of "not": "Man is like a thing of nought: his time passeth away like a shadow," Psalm 144.

(354,3)   It is often thought today that it was Henry Wriothesley (1573–1624) – the third Earl of Southampton, who was a friend of the second Earl of Essex (1565–1601) – who was Shakespeare's lover. At the end of the paragraph, Lacan is referring to a part of Sonnet 20:

> And for a woman wert thou first created,
> Till Nature as she wrought thee fell a-doting,
> And by addition me of thee defeated
> By adding one thing to my purpose nothing.
> But since she prick'd thee out for women's pleasure
> Mine be thy love, and thy love's use their treasure. [9–14]

XX   The Fundamental Fantasy

(358,7)   *Convoitise*: lusting after something.

(359,6)   Reading *chant* (song) instead of its homonym *champ* (field), as in section 2 below. *Chant du monde* (rendered here as "the way the world works") seems to metaphorically express the way things go or work, the way everyone thinks, or possibly the world's temptations.

(362,2)   I cannot locate anything in Glover's text that truly corresponds to Lacan's wording in quotes here. In the text we find the following: "the drug addict is able *to preserve his reality-sense from gross psychotic disturbance*" (p. 491); perverse ceremonials "*assisted in maintaining the patient's reality-sense to some degree*" (p. 493); and "perversions assist in preserving the amount of reality-sense already achieved by...." (p. 498). Perhaps this was not intended by Lacan to be a quotation at all. *Choses qui font flop* (things that flop) is *choses qui font floup* in the stenography, *floup* being an onomatopoeic word for a kind of dripping sound.

(363,1) Glover says that it is the drug addict who converts this first world into a chemist's shop.

(363,6) One might read *assurable* (can be ... assured) instead of *assumable* (can be ... taken up).

(364,1) See Heinz Hartmann's *Ego Psychology and the Problem of Adaptation*, trans. D. Rapaport (New York: International Universities Press, 1958), as well as his many articles in the *Psychoanalytic Quarterly* and the *International Journal of Psychoanalysis*.

(366,9) Recall that on the Graph of Desire, desire is situated on the right across from fantasy on the left.

(366,10) Assuming (or taking on) his own desire?

(368,1) "Shifter symbols": see Roman Jakobson, "Shifters, Verbal Categories, and the Russian Verb," in *Selected Writings,* vol. 2 (The Hague: Mouton, 1971), 130–47; and Lacan, *Écrits*, p. 448.

(370,4) Other versions include, in this table, a', a", and a'" instead of A', A", and A'".

(370,7) The grammar of the first sentence of this paragraph is quite problematic, there being few commas in the stenography that would clarify things: "*Disons que c'est pour autant qu'est introduite par le rapport le plus primordial du sujet le rapport de l'Autre, en tant que lieu de la parole, à la demande, que la dialectique s'institue....*"

"A divided by D": in France, long division is often carried out with the help of a table like the one Lacan provides here, instead of the kind used in the U.S., where this might be represented more or less as follows (where A is the dividend and D the divisor):

(371,1) "A signifying alternative": presumably, the presence/absence alternative.

(371,2) A reference to the lines at the beginning of Sonnet 45:

> The other two, slight air and purging fire,
> Are both with thee, wherever I abide;
> The first my thought, the other my desire,
> These present-absent with swift motion slide.

(371,4) One might read "strategy" here instead of "tragedy" (or "drama"), as in the next chapter.

(372,6) One might read *ses demandes* (his demands) instead of the homonymous *ces demandes* (these demands) twice in the first sentence of this paragraph.

(372,7) *Os* (hitch) could also be rendered by "rub" or "crux," and is a term sometimes used for "boner."

(373,2) See Matthew 16:25, Mark 8:35, Luke 9:24, and John 12:25. See, also, Juvenal's *Satires*, VIII, 83–4: *Summum crede nefas animam praeferre pudori et propter vitam vivendi perdere causas.* (Count it the greatest sin to prefer life to honor, and for the sake of living to lose what makes life worth living.)

(373,5) We might better read: "to which he is reduced" than "to which it is reduced."

XXI   In the Form of a Cut

(374,6) rA/S is not included in the table as we have it in the main body of the text. It should be included directly below A/D, as we see in the appendix (Table A.1).

(375,1) We might venture to write the mother as Other here as "mOther."

(375,5) Reading "strategy" instead of "tragedy," as found earlier in this paragraph and in other versions. It would be more grammatical in both French and English to say "recognized by the Other" instead of "recognized in the Other," but Lacan appears to have said *dans*; he uses *dans* at several other points in this class and subsequent classes as well when other prepositions would seem more likely.

(376,3) Again, reading "strategy" instead of "tragedy."

(376,5) *Au-delà* (beyond) also means hereafter.

(377,2) Other versions would have us read: "namely, from the imaginary register, from a part of himself that is involved in the imaginary relationship to the other."

(378,1) *Wo Es war, soll Ich werden* is from GW XV, p. 86, and corresponds to SE XXII, p. 80. Change "it" to "It."

(379,1) *Porté* ("borne along") could perhaps more felicitously be rendered here as "swept along."

(381,3) "Has come to occupy it": reading *l'a prise* instead of *l'a pris.*

(381,5) Change "itself" to "himself" in the last line of the paragraph.

(383,5) Change "cut off" to "cut off or taken away."

(387,1) Another version provides the neologism *signifiquantité,* "signifyquantity," instead of *signifiantiser.*

(387,2) Or "possible consecration vanishes in the signifying mark."

(388,4) We should probably read *Sie sollen nämlich* ... ("You were to ..."), as in *Écrits,* p. 452, instead of *Sie sollen werden....*

XXII Cut and Fantasy

(392,2) Lacan is referring here to a model he developed involving a camera photographing a mountain lake (see Seminar II, pp. 46–8), after the disappearance of all human beings from the planet. Miller suggests, in his appendix, that Lacan got the idea from Adolfo Bioy Casares's book *The Invention of Morel* (New York: New York Review Books, 1964 [original work published 1940]); see especially pp. 69–70.

(392,3) "Consciousness" should perhaps be understood here as "self-consciousness" or "self-awareness."

(392,6) Other versions suggest that the intentional loop is the entire horseshoe-shaped curve running from S to I(A); this would seem to be confirmed by the published version, for we read in Chap. 1 that, in Fig. 1.1, "the intentional process [...] runs from the id to capital I." See also Chap. 2.

(395,5) The French term *signifiance* which I generally translate as "signifierness," might also be translated as "significance," "signifyingness," "meaningfulness," "signifying nature," or even "signifying order" here (insofar as in the next paragraph Lacan virtually equates it with the Other). According to André Lalande's *Vocabulaire technique et critique de la philosophie* (Paris: PUF, 1976), the term was introduced into French linguistics in the 1960s, deriving from the English "significance," and is related to the English "connotation." According to the *Dictionnaire historique de la langue française* (Paris: Robert, 1994), "The word, which until recently was no longer in use, was taken up anew in the vocabulary of semiology and semiotics, designating (probably modeled on the English "significance") the fact of having meaning, opposed to *non signifiance.*" Lacan uses it to translate the *deutung* of Freud's *Traumdeutung* (*Écrits*, p. 520), which Strachey renders as "interpretation." In the course of Lacan's work, it takes on the meaning of "signifierness" or the "signifying nature" of signifiers – in other words, the sense in which the signifier dominates the signified. See, in particular, Lacan's "Instance of the Letter" (1957), where he equates it with *l'effet signifiant*, the signifying effect or signifier effect (*Écrits*, p. 441 n. 20).

Other versions read $s(A)$ here instead of $S(\cancel{A})$.

(396,3) See the parallel horizontal lines in Figure 13.1.

(397,2) Reading "compact," as in other versions, instead of "opaque."

(398,2) Lacan said "desire is the metonymy of the want-to-be" in *Écrits*, p. 520.

(401,3) Lacan said the English word "irrelevant," here and in the previous and the next few paragraphs, according to the stenography and other versions; he said the English word "relevant" according to the published edition, which is the term one finds in Eissler's text, although Eissler never defines a "relevant detail" as one that does not fit or make sense.

(401,8) All versions are somewhat erroneous as regards the first sentence of this paragraph, and the published version oddly asserts that, in the dream discussed at the beginning of the year, "The father knows he is dead and conveys this to his son."

(402,7) Lacan is paraphrasing a remark made by Einstein during his first visit to Princeton University (in April of 1921): "*Raffiniert ist der Herrgott, aber boshaft ist er nicht*," which is often rendered by "Subtle is the Lord, but malicious He is not." "God is subtle but He is not malicious" and "God is slick, but He ain't mean" are other translations that have been proposed.

(405,4) Change "jumps" to "leaps."

XXIII   The Function of the Subjective Slit in Perverse Fantasies

(414,2) See Seminar IV, pp. 88–92, and *Écrits*, pp. 509–10.

(414,5) Lebovici reports that "a man in armour attacks him from behind with a kind of gas mask, which brings to mind a fly spray and which would suffocate him." See Ruth Lebovici, "Perversion sexuelle transitoire au cours d'un traitement psychanalytique," *Bulletin d'activités de l'Association des Psychanalystes de Belgique*, 25 (1956): 1–15. In English, see "Transitory Sexual Perversion in the Course of a Psychoanalytic Treatment," trans. D. Nobus, in *Journal for Lacanian Studies* 2, *1* (2004): 118–40; see also *Studying Lacan's Seminars IV and V: From Lack to Desire*, eds. C. Owens and N. Chekurova (London: Routledge, 2018). Lebovici seems to think that it was a different interpretation she made, the one of his belief that his analysis could not end without him sleeping with the analyst, that led to perverse acting out. Lacan appears to accept this when he mentions the case again in Chapter XXIII.

(417,4) Other versions include the homonym *montré* (what is shown) instead of *montrer* (showing).

(419,3) An undine is a sort of mythological water spirit, nymph, or goddess. Cf. Seminar XXIV, *RSI* (class given on January 14, 1975).

(419,7) See Paul Valéry, *La Jeune Parque*, bilingual edition (Hexham, UK: Bloodaxe Books, 1997 [1917]).

(420,1)   "Only inasmuch as she is in fact the object of the exhibitionist's desire": other versions would have us read "only inasmuch as it is in fact the object of her desire."

XXIV   The Dialectic of Desire in Neurosis

(423,6)   See Lacan's use of *temps d'arrêt* in *Écrits*, p. 166.

(425,4)   *Passage à l'acte* is the French translation of the German *Agieren* (translated into English as "acting out") that was usual in the 1950s. See Daniel Lagache's translation of Melitta Schmideberg's "Note sur le transfert" ("Note on Transference") in *RFP* 16, *1–2* (1952): 263–7, especially p. 265, and the *Robert* dictionary under "*acte*." (Note, however, that Lacan begins to make a distinction between *passage à l'acte*—desperate act—and acting out later; see, for example, Seminar XIV, February 22, 1967.)

(425,5)   *Moment fécond* (fertile moment) may be related to Freud's term, "productive stage" of hysteria (see SE II, 17). Cf. Seminar III, p. 26, and *Écrits*, p. 147.

(426,1)   *L'approche de son désir* (desire's approach) is doubly ambiguous here. In this context, it likely means that the phobic object protects the subject from getting too close to the Other's desire (or stops the Other's desire from approaching him too closely), but it could also be to his own desire. Furthermore, Lacan often uses *son désir* as a shorthand for "the object of his desire," but it could even potentially mean (getting too close to) "realizing his desire."

Note that Lacan uses the verb *ouvrir* in this class in many different contexts and senses.

(431,2)   Reading V (for *vel*), as in the stenography and other versions, instead of tilde (~). The tilde in logic is a symbol for negation, not disjunction.

XXV   The Either/Or Concerning the Object

(437,2)   *Vertu dormitive* (soporific value) is from Molière's *The Imaginary Invalid*, where it is used in reference to opium.

(438,6) It is not clear to me what Lacan means by *momentalité*. Could it be a play on words between moment (or stage) and mentality, refer to being short-lived, or to being in the moment? It seems to have been used very occasionally by French authors over the years, but I can find no definition of it.

(440,5) Lacan appears here to be interpreting Klein's discussion on the bottom half of p. 33.

(443,7) Reading *Rückphantasie* instead of *Rück-Phantasie*. The term was used by Wilhelm Stekel in his book *Sadism and Masochism*. It is, however, likely that what Lacan actually said was *Zurückphantasieren*, which is Freud's term for "retrospective fantasy" (SE IV, p. 288; SE VII, p. 103 n; and elsewhere).

(445,2) *Crasia* is a Greek suffix meaning power or rule.

(445,5) "Although he may even be nowhere in it": other versions read "although he cannot be anywhere [in particular] in it."

(446,3) At the first session, Dick simply said, "Nurse?" Klein replied, "Nurse is soon coming," and at the next session he said, "Nurse coming?"

(446,4) Klein mentions his "physical awkwardness" (p. 27) and says he was lacking in "coordination" (p. 27) and "clumsy in all his movements" (p. 29). Klein says that the object cut with the scissors is "a little coal-cart" made of wood, not that it is part of the train he has begun playing with. Dick asks her to cut a piece of (wood that represents) coal off it, she gives him the scissors, "but he could not hold the scissors. Acting on a glance which he gave me, I cut the pieces of wood out of the cart, whereupon he threw the damaged cart and its contents into a drawer and said, 'Gone'" (p. 31).

(446,5) The *Carte du Tendre* is a seventeenth-century map of the tender/amorous sentiments—perhaps a forerunner to Adam Smith's (1759) *Theory of Moral Sentiments*—drawn by Madeleine de Scudéry. It purported to trace out all the stages of love, all the stages of the development of affection, as well as all the obstacles and problems one might encounter along love's path, such as jealousy and despair. It can be found in her ten-volume novel *Clélie* (1654–60). The map can be found in Joan DeJean's

Tender Geographies: Women and the Origins of the Novel in France (New York: Columbia University Press, 1991).

Lacan seems to be distinguishing this from a "tender" or "tender offer," an offer or proposal to exchange one thing for another, to pay off a debt, etc.

(446,7) Lacan mistakenly said *poitrine* (chest) instead of *genoux* or *giron* (lap), as in Klein's paper. Klein mentions "empathy" here, but not "panic."

(447,1) "By attempting to obtain a reduction of his desires to his needs": certain analysts today seem to have adopted a different strategy: instead of reducing patients' desires to their needs, they simply set out to satisfy them!

(447,2) Or: "everything we theorize boils down to what I say [to him]."

(448,2) "To really have it in a man": the words "in a man" are found only in the published text.

(449,6) "Consider my little illustration of demand:" other versions include the following abbreviated table:

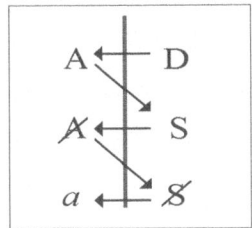

(450,6) "Zone of the object": the grey zone in Figure 25.1.

XXVI The Function of Splitting* in Perversion

(454,3) Other versions add at the end of this first sentence: "where reality [*réel*] is at stake."

(454,8) Change "seal" to "seal [or: stamp, *seau*]."

(458,4) Cronus, a Titan, castrated his father, Uranus, and was in turn castrated by his own son, Zeus.

(460,4) *Life, Death and Sex: Selected Writings of William Gillespie* (London: Routledge, 1995).

(460,5) The French in the first sentence of this paragraph is very unclear in all versions, and the grammar is less than adequate. I have done my best to follow Gillespie's case study.

(463,1) What Gide actually said is not, "Vous ne savez pas ce qu'est l'amour d'un uraniste," as we find it in the published Seminar, but "Personne ne peut soupçonner ce qu'est l'amour d'un uraniste: quelque chose de si fort, de si bien préservé, quelque chose d'embaumé contre quoi le temps n'a plus prise…."; the quote can be found in Jean Schlumberger, *Madeleine et André Gide* (Paris: Gallimard, 1956), p. 193. Cf. *Écrits*, p. 635.

(463,4) The passages by Gide here are from *If It Die…: An Autobiography* (New York: Random House/Vintage, 2001 [1935]).

(465,1) Reading *refente* (split) instead of *fente* (slit), the word "slit" appearing nowhere in Gillespie's writings, to the best of my knowledge.

(465,2) See Freud's "Psychogenesis of a Case of Homosexuality in a Woman" (SE XVIII, pp. 147–72) and Lacan's commentary on it in Seminar IV, Chaps. 6–8.

(465,6) Φ should perhaps be barred here, as it is on page 452.

(466,2) Again reading *refente* (split) instead of *fente* (slit), the word "slit" appearing nowhere in Gillespie's writings, to the best of my knowledge.

XXVII Toward Sublimation

(471,6) Much of the literature Lacan was reading at the time, including Lebovici's article, talks about *névroses de caractère*, "character neuroses"; Lacan perhaps loosely translated that term as *caractères névrotiques*, which literally means neurotic characters or traits, but we might think here of neurotic character structures or what are today often referred to as personality, character, or characterological disorders.

(475,1) Change "unanswered" to "unmet." In the next sentence, change "answer" to "meet."

(475,3) *Distorsion du moi*: see *Écrits*, p. 542 n. 16.

(476,3) *Poussée* (pressure) is the usual translation of Freud's *Drang*, one of the components of the drive; see SE XIV, p. 122. The other components of the drive are its aim, object, and source. In the next paragraph, Lacan seems to translate aim as *tendance*, which might also be understood as trend or drift.

(476,4) Change "[or: (pre)disposition" to "[or: aim or (pre)disposition."

(478,7) Although Miller indicates in his appendix that the poem runs as follows–

J'ai vu le Diable, l'autre nuit ;
Et, dessous sa pelure,
Il n'est pas aisé de conclure
S'il faut dire : Elle, ou : Lui.

–in the body of the text we find that Lacan apparently added a line of his own:

J'ai vu le Diable, l'autre nuit ;
Et, dessous sa pelure,
Il dépassait ses deux….

(481,5) Lebovici writes, "We told him that he was playing a game of making himself afraid of an event which he knew would never happen."

See Maurice Bouvet, "La clinique psychanalytique. La relation d'objet," in *La psychanalyse d'aujourd'hui* (Paris: PUF, 1956); see Lacan's comments on Bouvet in *Écrits*, pp. 508–9, and in S4, Chaps. 1 and 2. I cannot find anything in Lebovici's case study that justifies what Lacan claims in the next paragraph.

(482,3) Lacan has misunderstood Kris's text here, as I explain in detail in *Lacan to the Letter* (Minneapolis, MN: University of Minnesota Press, 2004), pp. 52–62; moreover, he did not discuss Kris's text in "Function in Field," but rather in "Response to Jean Hyppolite's Commentary on Freud's '*Verneinung*'" (*Écrits*, pp. 328–32); he corrects some of the points he gets wrong here in the published version of "Direction of the Treatment."

(486,4) Viardot constructed *grain de fantaisie* like *grain de beauté* (beauty mark), but *un grain de* also means a bit, hint, or touch of (thus, a touch of beauty).

(486,7) In the same poem by Viardot, we find "Les femmes ont dans la fente un grain de poésie."

Appendix

(491,4) Canguilhem's "second thesis": up until the 1960s, one wrote a doctoral thesis and could then write a second thesis to qualify for the highest degree in France: *la these d'état*.

(493,5) See Miller's comments on Christine Angot at: https://laregledujeu.org/2013/03/08/12695/%C2%AB-il-sait-bien-des-tours-le-renard-le-herisson-n%E2%80%99en-connait-qu%E2%80%99un-mais-il-est-fameux-%C2%BB/.

(504,3) Father Ubu is a character in Alfred Jarry's play *Ubu Roi ou les polonais* (Paris: Eugène Fasquelle, [1888] 1922); in English see *King Turd* (New York: Boar's Head Books, 1953).

(504,5) "Dossier pédagogique": see http://studylibfr.com/doc/6097031/ubu-encha%C3%AEn%C3%A9-1—-acad%C3%A9mie-de-caen.

(507,1) Reading *Lectures on the History of Philosophy* instead of *Lectures on the Philosophy of History*.

(511,2) "Lacan's version of communism": here is the sentence from *Écrits*, p. 264: "But we can simultaneously see that the dialectic is not individual, and that the question of the termination of an analysis is that of the moment at which the subject's satisfaction is achievable in the satisfaction of all—that is, of all those it involves in a human undertaking."

(517,4) I have slightly corrected the poem based on the version found in *Les Contrerimes* (Paris: Gallimard, 1979), p. 70.

(519)   Add "being, 408" before "Being and the One."

(520)   Add "communism, 411" after "comedy."

Bibliography of Lacan's Seminars Cited

Lacan, J. (1953–1977). The Seminars cited here in order:

1. *The Seminar of Jacques Lacan, Book I: Freud's Papers on Technique (1953–1954)*. J.-A. Miller (Ed.), J. Forrester (Trans.). New York: W. W. Norton, 1988.
2. *The Seminar of Jacques Lacan, Book II: The Ego in Freud's Theory and in the Technique of Psychoanalysis (1954–1955)*. J.-A. Miller (Ed.), S. Tomaselli (Trans.). New York: W. W. Norton, 1988.
3. *The Seminar of Jacques Lacan, Book III: The Psychoses (1955–1956)*. J.-A. Miller (Ed.), R. Grigg (Trans.). New York: W. W. Norton, 1993.
4. *Le séminaire, Livre IV: La relation d'objet*. Paris: Seuil, 1994.
5. *The Seminar of Jacques Lacan, Book V: Formations of the Unconscious (1957–1958)*. J.-A. Miller (Ed.), R. Grigg (Trans.). Cambridge: Polity, 2017.
6. *The Seminar of Jacques Lacan, Book VI: Desire and Its Interpretation (1958–1959)*. J.-A. Miller (Ed.), B. Fink (Trans.). Cambridge: Polity, 2019.
7. *The Seminar of Jacques Lacan, Book VII: The Ethics of Psychoanalysis (1959–1960)*. J.-A. Miller (Ed.), D. Porter (Trans.). New York: W. W. Norton, 1992.

© The Author(s), under exclusive license to Springer Nature Switzerland AG 2025 **193**
B. Fink, *Lacan on Desire*, The Palgrave Lacan Series,
https://doi.org/10.1007/978-3-031-76386-1

8. *The Seminar of Jacques Lacan, Book VIII: Transference (1960–1961)*. J.-A. Miller (Ed.), B. Fink (Trans.). Cambridge: Polity, 2015.

9. *Le séminaire, Livre X: L'angoisse*. Paris: Seuil, 2004.

10. *The Seminar of Jacques Lacan, Book XI: The Four Fundamental Concepts of Psychoanalysis*. J.-A. Miller (Ed.), A. Sheridan (Trans.). New York: W. W. Norton, 1978.

11. *Le séminaire, Livre XIV: La logique du fantasme*. Paris: Seuil, 2023.

12. *Le séminaire, Livre XV: L'Acte psychanalytique*. Paris: Seuil, 2024.

13. *The Seminar of Jacques Lacan, Book XVI: From an Other to the other (1968–1969)*. J.-A. Miller (Ed.), B. Fink (Trans.). Cambridge: Polity, 2023.

14. *The Seminar of Jacques Lacan, Book XVIII: On a Discourse that Might Not Be a Semblance (1970–1971)*. J.-A. Miller (Ed.), B. Fink (Trans.). Cambridge: Polity, 2025.

15. *The Seminar of Jacques Lacan, Book XX: Encore (1972–1973)*. J.-A. Miller (Ed.), B. Fink (Trans.). New York: W. W. Norton, 1998.

16. *Le séminaire, Livre XXIII: Le sinthome*. Paris: Seuil, 2005.

17. *Le séminaire, Livre XXIV: L'insu que sait de l'une-bévue s'aile à mourre (1976–1977)*. (Unpublished).

References

Collins, D. (2022)."Hamlet and Reality Testing." Paper presented in Russell Grigg's seminar *Lacan Goes to the Theatre*, Melbourne, Australia, on September 10, 2022.

Falzeder, E. (1994). "My grand-patient, my chief tormentor: A hitherto unnoticed case of Freud's and the consequences." *Psychoanalytic Quarterly,* 63: 297–331.

Fink, B. (1991). "There's No Such Thing as a Sexual Relationship: Existence and the Formulas of Sexuation" in *Newsletter of the Freudian Field* 5.

Fink, B. (1995). *The Lacanian Subject: Between Language and Jouissance.* Princeton, NJ: Princeton University Press.

Fink, B. (1997). *A Clinical Introduction to Lacanian Psychoanalysis: Theory and Technique.* Cambridge, MA: Harvard University Press.

Fink, B. (2004). *Lacan to the Letter: Reading* Écrits *Closely.* Minneapolis, MN: University of Minnesota Press.

Fink, B. (2010). *The Adventures of Inspector Canal* (London: Karnac)

Fink, B. (2014a). *Against Understanding: Vol. 1. Commentary and Critique in a Lacanian Key.* London: Routledge.

Fink, B. (2014b). *Against Understanding: Vol. 2. Cases and Commentary in a Lacanian Key.* London: Routledge.

Fink, B. (2016). *Lacan on Love: An Exploration of Lacan's Seminar VIII,* Transference. Cambridge: Polity.

Fink, B. (2024). *Miss-ing: Psychoanalysis 2.0*. London: Aeon.

Freud, S. (1953–1974). *The Standard Edition of the Complete Psychological Works of Sigmund Freud* (Vols. I–XXIV). London: Hogarth.

Jones, E. (1961). "Early Development of Female Sexuality" (first published in 1927), in *Papers on Psycho-Analysis*, 5th edition. Boston: Beacon.

Lacan, J. (1968). "Proposition du 9 octobre 1967 sur le psychanalyste de l'école," in *Scilicet* 1.

Lacan, J. (1973). *Le séminaire, Livre XI: Les quatre concepts fondamentaux de la psychanalyse*. Paris: Seuil.

Lacan, J. (1973–1974). *Le séminaire, Livre XXI: Les non dupes errent*. (Unpublished).

Lacan, J. (1974–1975). *Le séminaire, Livre XXII: RSI*. (Unpublished).

Lacan, J. (1975). *Le séminaire, Livre XX: Encore*. Paris: Seuil.

Lacan, J. (1976–1977). *Le séminaire, Livre XXIV: L'insu que sait de l'une-bévue s'aile à mourre*. (Unpublished).

Lacan, J. (1978). *The Seminar of Jacques Lacan, Book XI: The Four Fundamental Concepts of Psychoanalysis*. J.-A. Miller (Ed.), A. Sheridan (Trans.). New York: W. W. Norton.

Lacan, J. (1988a). *The Seminar of Jacques Lacan, Book I: Freud's Papers on Technique (1953–1954)*. J.-A. Miller (Ed.), J. Forrester (Trans.). New York: W. W. Norton.

Lacan, J. (1988b). *The Seminar of Jacques Lacan, Book II: The Ego in Freud's Theory and in the Technique of Psychoanalysis (1954–1955)*. J.-A. Miller (Ed.), S. Tomaselli (Trans.). New York: W. W. Norton.

Lacan, J. (1992). *The Seminar of Jacques Lacan, Book VII: The Ethics of Psychoanalysis (1959–1960)*. J.-A. Miller (Ed.), D. Porter (Trans.). New York: W. W. Norton.

Lacan, J. (1993). *The Seminar of Jacques Lacan, Book III: The Psychoses (1955–1956)*. J.-A. Miller (Ed.), R. Grigg (Trans.). New York: W. W. Norton.

Lacan, J. (1994). *Le séminaire, Livre IV: La relation d'objet*. Paris: Seuil.

Lacan, J. (1998). *The Seminar of Jacques Lacan, Book XX: Encore (1972–1973)*. J.-A. Miller (Ed.), B. Fink (Trans.). New York: W. W. Norton.

Lacan, J. (2001). *Autres Écrits*. Paris: Seuil.

Lacan, J. (2004). *Le séminaire, Livre X: L'angoisse*. Paris: Seuil.

Lacan, J. (2006). *Écrits: The First Complete Edition in English*. B. Fink (Trans.). New York: W. W. Norton. (Original work published 1966.)

Lacan, J. (2015). *The Seminar of Jacques Lacan, Book VIII: Transference (1960–1961)*. J.-A. Miller (Ed.), B. Fink (Trans.). Cambridge: Polity.

Lacan, J. (2019). *The Seminar of Jacques Lacan, Book VI: Desire and Its Interpretation (1958–1959)*. J.-A. Miller (Ed.), B. Fink (Trans.). Cambridge: Polity.

Lacan, J. (2023). *The Seminar of Jacques Lacan, Book XVI: From an Other to the other (1968–1969)*. J.-A. Miller (Ed.), B. Fink (Trans.). Cambridge: Polity.

Lacan, J. (2025). *The Seminar of Jacques Lacan, Book XVIII: On a Discourse that Might Not Be a Semblance (1970–1971)*. J.-A. Miller (Ed.), B. Fink (Trans.). Cambridge: Polity.

Lagache, D. (1956). "Deuil pathologique" in *La Psychanalyse* 2: 45–74.

Maleval, J.-C. (2021). *La Différence autistique*. Saint Denis: Presses Universitaires de Vincennes.

Malpass, A. and Marfori, M. A. (2017). *The History of Philosophical and Formal Logic: From Aristotle to Tarski*. London and New York: Bloomsbury Academic.

Sharpe, E. F. (1937). *Dream Analysis*. London: The Hogarth Press and the Institute of Psycho-Analysis.

Index[1]

---

[1] Note: Page numbers followed by 'n' refer to notes.

The manufacturer's authorised representative in the EU is Springer
Nature Customer Service Centre GmbH, Europaplatz 3, 69115 Heidelberg,
Germany. If you have any concerns regarding our products, please
contact ProductSafety@springernature.com

Printed and bound by CPI Group (UK) Ltd, Croydon, CR0 4YY

29/04/2026

02099544-0001